GOLF: The Body, the Mind, the Game

answers the following (and many other) questions that will help you reach your full golfing potential.

For distance, what is the one thing *all PGA Tour pros do that amateurs do not?*

Specifically, *how do you replace negative feelings and perceptions with their positive counterparts?*

What is the single action that makes sand shots easy?

Why should you learn to think about "turning" rather than "swinging"?

What is a "gravity shot"? Why is it a key to scoring?

What are the 5 Winning Rules for dealing successfully with mental pressure?

Why do the vast majority of golfers who take lessons, read books and magazines, and buy high-tech equipment not improve?

Why do the longest Tour hitters have most of their weight on the right side at impact?

For practice to be meaningful, what three tenets should be followed?

Why is it imperative to accelerate the putter head on the through stroke? How do you do this correctly?

How important is it to have the same routine for all standard shots?

What is the "Good Hit Instinct"?

How do you learn to use one thought *to the exclusion of all others during shot making?*

GOLF

VILLARD • NEW YORK • 1995

GOLF

THE BODY,

THE MIND,

THE GAME

DICK BEACH AND BOB FORD

All rights reserved under International and Pan-American
Copyright Conventions. Published in the United States by
Villard Books, a division of Random House, Inc., New York,
and simultaneously in Canada by Random House of Canada
Limited, Toronto.

An earlier edition of this work was self-published by the author in 1992.

Villard Books is a registered trademark of Random House, Inc.

Library of Congress Cataloging-in-Publication Data
Beach, Dick.
     Golf: the body, the mind, the game / by
Dick Beach and Bob Ford.
          p.   cm.
     Includes bibliographical references.
     ISBN 0-679-43958-7
     1. Golf.   2. Golf—Psychological aspects.   I. Ford, Bob.
II. Title.
GV965.B37   1995
796.352—dc20   94-47544

Manufactured in the United States of America on acid-free paper

98765432

First Villard Books Edition

*To Julie,
without whose
encouragement
this book would
never have been
started*

ACKNOWLEDGMENTS

For technical information and sound advice we are especially indebted to Lynda Shirley and Bruce McGough. For their incisive comments as well as constant enthusiasm and support we give special thanks to Lisa Beach and Christopher Heinz.

CONTENTS

Acknowledgments   *ix*
Uncle Charlie   *xiii*
Introduction   *xv*
Glossary   *xvii*

I. THE PHYSICAL GAME   *1*

1. EXERCISES   *4*
2. GRIP AND ADDRESS   *15*
3. THE GOLF MOVEMENT: TURNBACK, TRANSITION,
    TURNTHROUGH   *21*
4. GREENSIDE PLAY   *41*
5. SAND PLAY   *48*
6. ALTERED SHOTS   *54*
7. ROUTINE, PRACTICE   *60*
8. TEACHING, LEARNING   *68*

II. THE MENTAL GAME   *75*

9.   THE BRAIN   *79*
10. THE LEARNING STAGE—STAGE I   *82*
11. A SINGLE THOUGHT—STAGE II   *84*
12. PERCEPTIONS, FEELINGS, ATTITUDES   *93*

13. CONFIDENCE   *101*
14. ASSURANCE—STAGE III   *110*

III. PUTTING   *117*

15. PREPARATION   *119*
16. PUTTING ABSOLUTES   *124*
17. THE PUTTING STROKE   *129*
18. THE MENTAL GAME   *135*
19. PUTTING WITH CONFIDENCE   *139*

IV. FINAL THOUGHTS   *143*

20. A WORD ON WINNING   *145*
21. CONCLUSION   *152*

Bibliography   *154*
Recommended Videos   *157*

UNCLE CHARLIE

Everybody knows an Uncle Charlie. Before breakfast he downs a "little shooter"—about two ounces of whiskey that Charlie says "jump-starts the ol' ticker."

For breakfast, he eats what he has always eaten: fried eggs, bacon, butter-laden toast, and fried potatoes. After breakfast, Charlie lights up the first of about a dozen black stogies he will smoke that day.

Lunch is three very dry martinis followed by an oversized Reuben. For dinner, Charlie has steak and potatoes with a rich, sugary dessert and, of course, a few drinks—before, during, and after.

Charlie has a health checkup every year. The doctor's report is like a broken record: "Cholesterol below 200. HDL, LDL, and triglycerides are perfect. In short, Charlie, you're healthy as a horse." Never in his life has Charlie been hospitalized.

Uncle Charlie is seventy-eight years old and frequently "shoots his age" on the golf course.

For every statement made in this book, there will be an Uncle Charlie out there—someone who does just the opposite and is still successful. This book is for the other 99 percent.

If you're an "Uncle Charlie" who does nothing by the book but still plays a great game of golf, God bless you.

INTRODUCTION

Golf, like all sports, has two parts—the physical and the mental. Learning to master each, and having them function in harmony, is what makes golf so difficult. This is reflected in two common phrases that are accurate but rarely explained: "Golf is an unnatural game" and "Golf is 90 percent mental."

Here is what "Golf is an unnatural game" means: Think of any sport where the player must throw, catch, push, pull, hit, or swing. From the start to the finish, the player's dominant side is active and in charge. The shoulder, arm, and hand move as a unit back and then forward. This is the natural thing to do. To play correctly, however, the golfer must overcome this dominant-side instinct—the urge to take the club back and drive it down to hit the ball. He or she must keep this area passive until well into the forward movement, when its stored energy is released.

The successful golfer accomplishes this by turning his body mass away from the ball rather than having the arms and hands swing the club back. This is a "getting-set" move called the *Turnback*. The active lower body generates the forward movement. This is called the *Turnthrough*. The arms, hands, and club do not actively swing; they are passively swung.

Once this concept is understood, learned, and used, the

player is well on the way to playing a correct and consistent golf game. This book will show you how to accomplish that.

Your own experiences will surely confirm that "golf is 90 percent mental." How else can you account for your good shots on the practice tee and your inability to reproduce them on the course? How else can you reconcile well-played shots followed by misses using the same club? This inconsistency of play is strictly mental. Yet, knowing that golf is more than 90 percent mental is not the problem. Learning how to deal successfully with this phenomenon is. This book will give you the complete solution to that problem.

You might think that having a correct physical game and a correct mental game is sufficient to play great golf. It is not. It is only when each of these two parts performs synchronously and in harmony that you make consistent, quality shots. This book fully explains the means to accomplish this synthesis.

GLOSSARY

Absolutes: Required actions for achieving shot consistency and success.

Contra: The simultaneous but opposite actions of the *Unit* and lower body during the *Transition*.

Golf Movement: The total physical action, composed of the *Turnback*, the *Transition*, and the *Turnthrough*.

Transition: The time during which the body and then the *Unit* changes direction.

Turnback: That part of the *Golf Movement* commonly referred to as the "backswing" or the "take-away."

Turnthrough: The turning-forward action following the *Turnback*.

Unit: The shoulders, arms, hands, and golf club functioning as one.

Variables: The opposite of *Absolutes*. Actions that vary from person to person but do not prevent making a successful, consistent shot.

1.

THE PHYSICAL GAME

Picture in your mind the athletes performing the hammer throw, the discus toss, and the javelin throw. Their goal is to propel an object the maximum distance— with accuracy. This is accomplished by creating an axis—the spine. The turning body rotates around this axis. Power comes from body torque and peaks in the sequence: lower body, upper body, arms, hands, wrists at the moment of release.

This is also, basically, how the **Golf Movement** *is performed.*

INTRODUCTION

The physical golf game is composed of two parts: preparation and action.

Description of the preparation, grip, and address differs little from one golf writer to another.

It is in the action, the playing of the shot, that we take you, the reader, on a different path.

This is a journey you will enjoy.

The innovations will move your knowledge of the game to a higher level: They are meaningful, correct, and complete. More important, they will show you how to achieve the maximum distance and accuracy at your current skill level. Finally, you will learn the formula for capturing golf's most elusive prize—consistency-of-quality play.

As Phil Mickelson said, "This book describes how to play the game of golf differently than you have ever heard or seen before."

Chapter 1

EXERCISES

The next few exercises will introduce you to the concept of the *Golf Movement*. Although they may seem simplistic or irrelevant, they provide a critical basis of understanding for the entire *Golf Movement*.

Exercise 1

For distance shots, the body plays a major role. An arms-dominant swing is not enough.

Wad a piece of paper and stand facing a target 10 feet away. Relax. Toss the paper underhand at the target. This is an arm movement; any slight body motion is incidental.

Now try a longer toss of 20 to 30 feet. The body motion is no longer incidental. For this distance, you need body effort to hit your target. Try to toss the wadded paper using only your arm and hand. No success? The paper wad is off its mark, probably short.

THE BODY MUST LEAD, THE ARM FOLLOWS

Here's a full golf-shot exercise illustrating that the turning body is the basic and essential feature of the entire *Golf Movement.* A golf club is not used for this exercise.

Exercise 2

1. Stand with your feet apart (about shoulder width) and your weight evenly balanced.
2. Bend your knees, lowering your buttocks a few inches.
3. Relax. Shrug your shoulders to relax them.
4. Straighten your spine and lean forward slightly from the hips. Chin up.
5. *Fold your arms across your chest.* You are ready to begin the *Turnback.*

In one level motion, turn your legs, hips, torso, and shoulders to the right. Your right leg must *not* straighten. If your right leg straightens on the *Turnback,* your pelvis will tilt, causing the upper body and shoulders to tilt downward. This awkward position will offset the *Turnback* and, consequently, trying to recover from this position to begin the *Turnthrough* nearly always results in failure.

Turning your body mass to the right will naturally cause the majority of your weight to go to the right side.

Allow your left heel to lift in order to make turning easier.

Do not "slide" your hips. Turn them.

When your shoulders have turned about 90 degrees and your hips about half of that, the *Turnback* is completed. Relax and hold this position. If you *turned* back and did not *slide* back, your right hip is inside the outer edge of your right shoe.

The *Turnthrough* is sequential (as opposed to the all-together motion of the *Turnback*). Generate this forward movement by turning your hips to the left. Your torso and shoulders will naturally follow. Your left leg is extended and your right heel comes off the ground as you finish, facing your target.

At the finish, your hips will not have passed the out-side of your left foot.

Repeat this exercise until you have developed a strong sense of your body turning in each direction and of the weight naturally moving with it. You will soon become com-fortable with the basic concept of the correct *Golf Move-ment:*

The Body Turns

Before you begin Exercise 3, note the way, ideally, in which the club head tracks on an invisible plane, extending from the ball through the shoulders.

To make a perfect shot every time, the club head would have to travel on exactly the same plane and the same orbit in each direction. Iron Byron, the golf-ball striking and test-ing machine, does just that. For a human to replicate such precision is impossible. Each time you swing the club back, your right arm folds. Since your right arm remains folded well into the *Turnthrough,* a new orbit is created for the club head. There are two orbits but, ideally, only one plane dur-ing the total *Movement* (Illustration 1).

If your arms and hands are allowed to direct the club, each swing will be random. There will be no structure and thus no control.

For the club head to remain on the correct plane and scribe the correct arcs, you need to do three things: Turn correctly, maintain an extended left arm, and keep your upper right arm close to your body.

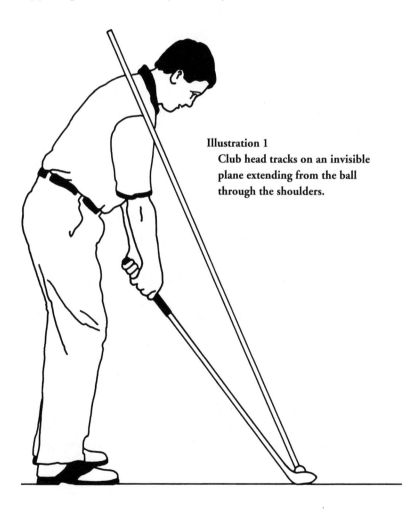

Illustration 1
   Club head tracks on an invisible plane extending from the ball through the shoulders.

Exercise 3

Exercise 3 is the same as Exercise 2 except that instead of folding your arms across your chest, you use a golf club.

Take your address position and begin the *Turnback* as you did in the previous exercise. This time, the *Unit* is included in the fluid motion. Be conscious of the actively turning body swinging the passive *Unit.* Along the upward path, the weight of the club will cause your relaxed wrists to begin cocking. Allow the club to coast to its apex.

Begin the *Turnthrough* by turning your lower body to the left while keeping the *Unit* in the same posture it had at the *Turnback* apex. This move will cause your hands to be lowered to about waist height. Your wrists will still be fully cocked and the club will be pointed skyward. At this point your wrists must (and will instinctively) uncock to send the club head through the ball position. Momentum will cause your body to come up and around so your face and torso are directed at the target.

Repeat this exercise a number of times until it is one continuous movement and you are aware that

The Turning Body Swings the Unit

This brings us to that long-held and erroneous belief that the club head's downward path goes "inside to outside" of the ball flight path.

The ball flight path is a line that extends from the target back through the ball position and continues to a point just past the golfer. Everything from that line to the golfer is "inside." Everything on the other side of the line is "outside." From the address position, the club head can only move on an inside path on its backward-upward track (Illustration 2).

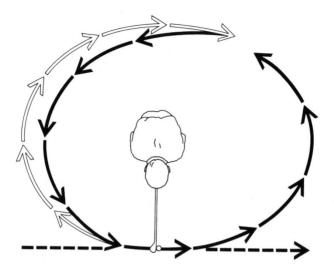

Illustration 2
  Club head remains *inside* for
  the entire *Golf Movement.*

Your lower body turning toward the target initiates the downward/forward action. This is, in effect, a "clearing-out" action. Your fully cocked wrists are lowered to a position opposite your waist area. Your right arm is close to your body; your right elbow brushes your right hip. Your hips are still turning counterclockwise as the club head impacts the ball. This combination of actions demands that the club head continue through the ball, down the target line, and then move with your body in a counterclockwise direction.

The Path of the Golf Club Is Totally "Inside to Inside"

These three exercises clearly demonstrate that *the turning body is the activator.*

Don't think this phenomenon is unique to hitting a golf ball. Regard it, correctly, as the way in which a person can send an object the maximum distance with directional accuracy. For example, remember learning to skip flat stones across a pond: The first thing you did was pick up a flat stone and just throw it. Because you threw only with your arm, the stone sank after a few bounces. When you learned the body came first, then the arm, and finally the wrist snap, you were ready to play the game.

The same concept applies to making a golf shot. In one motion, turn your body away from the target. Turn back to the target in sequence: lower body, upper body, and arms, and, finally, uncock your wrists.

Another good example of "the turning body swinging the *Unit*" is seen in home-run hitters.

The batter must hit the ball within a limited time frame. He begins his move at a point that corresponds to the apex of the *Turnback.* Most of his weight is on his back foot, his wrists are fully cocked, his knees are bent. He is in a set-and-ready position to begin the *Turnthrough* when the pitcher throws the ball (Illustration 3).

When the batter begins his *Turnthrough,* he steps forward and twists his hips to face the pitcher (Illustration 4). This causes a lower-body weight shift and establishes a brace with his extended leg and hip. Except for the fact that the golfer does not move his feet from the original placement, his actions are similar. The batter's body torque brings the bat to the ready position. His wrists, fully cocked, uncock to drive the bat through the ball and send it up, up, and away.

Watching these hitters, you will see *Variables* and *Absolutes. Variables* for the batters are in stance and bat position; how he stands or whether he holds the bat high or

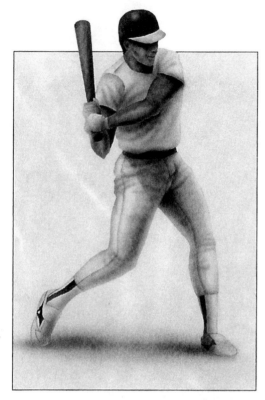

Illustration 3
- Weight is on back foot
- Knees are bent
- Wrists are fully cocked
- The player is set and ready

low is of little consequence. His success is based on how he executes the *Absolutes: Turnback* and *Turnthrough.*

SUMMARY

The *Golf Movement* consists of a *Turnback* and a *Turnthrough.*

The *Turnback* swings your *Unit* (shoulders, arms, hands, club) back and upward.

Illustration 4
- Lower body is active and leads
- Player strides forward and twists hips
- Extended leg and hip form a brace
- Wrists uncock to impact

The *Turnthrough* swings your *Unit* down and forward to a finish.

Your *Unit* moves only when swung by your turning body.

The action of your arms/hands is dependent, not independent.

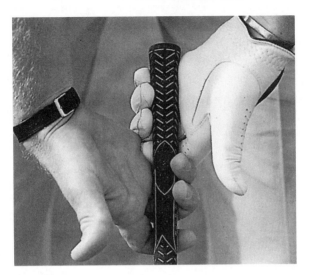

Illustration 5

- The club rests totally in the left index finger and then moves diagonally back across the palm

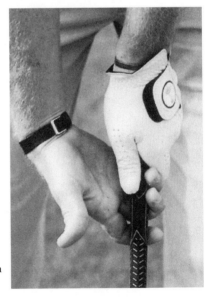

Illustration 6

- Left thumb points straight down
- Line between thumb and index finger points between chin and right shoulder

Chapter 2

GRIP AND ADDRESS

GRIP

Building a solid foundation for the *Golf Movement* is as necessary as building a solid foundation for a house. If you don't, you will have serious problems down the road, regardless of how well the rest of the structure (or the game) is put together.

Illustration 7
- **Right thumb points down**
- **Index finger does not touch middle finger**
- **Index finger forms a "7"; the base goes straight down—middle goes 90°— tip points back to body**
- **Line between thumb and index finger points between chin and right shoulder**

Accepting that the hands function as one entity, you use either an interlocking or overlapping grip. With the interlocking grip, the right little finger interlocks with the left pointer finger. With the overlapping grip, the right little finger overlaps the space between the left pointer and middle fingers.

Facing a golfer, you would see a "line" running from between the left thumb and pointer finger to between the chin and right shoulder. The left thumb points straight down or slightly to the right of the club shaft. Most players have their left hand on the shaft correctly. Those who do not are able to make the required adjustments easily.

When a grip problem exists, it is almost always due to the position of the right hand, which is usually stronger and accustomed to "taking charge." A so-called strong grip may be easier and feel more natural, but it is wrong. With this grip, the right hand is "under" the shaft, the middle and ring fingernails can be seen, and the pointer finger touches the middle finger.

With the strong grip, the club face *must* turn and open as the club moves away from the ball. To hit the ball correctly, the club face must turn back the exact amount it opened and at precisely the right instant. If it doesn't close enough and the face is still open at impact, the ball will travel to the right. If it closes too soon, the ball will hook and/or pull to the left.

To demonstrate this, hold a club with your right hand only. Use a strong grip and place the club head on the ground as you would at address. Bending your elbow, lift the club straight back over your head. What did the club face do? It turned to the right and opened. It had to in order to allow the wrist to bend.

Now try the same demonstration with the correct right-hand grip.

Turn your right hand to the left so that your thumb is on the top left quadrant. Your middle and ring fingernails should not be visible. Your pointer finger does not touch your middle finger but goes down the shaft; it forms a number "7" where the base is straight, the top is straight, and the end tip goes back toward your body. The V-line between thumb and index finger points to a spot between the chin and right shoulder.

Bending your elbow, lift the club straight back over your head. What did the club-face angle do this time? It remained exactly as it was at address: square to the swing circle line. A correct right-hand position will keep the club face square to the swing circle line during the entire back-and-forward movement. The result: The club face moves squarely through the ball at impact—every time. You will have achieved consistency.

This simple change in grip has dramatically improved the game for thousands of golfers.

ALIGNMENT

Prior to addressing the ball, make certain that body and club alignment are correct. Most golfers unintentionally align to the right of their target. You can prevent this by developing the following routine and using it for all full shots.

1. Approach the ball from behind the ball-to-target flight line, not from the side.
2. Visualize the flight path the ball will take to reach the target.

3. Place the club head behind the ball. Look at the target again to make sure the club head is square to the flight line.

4. Set your left foot and then your right foot—in that order. This sequence of club-face alignment, left foot first, right foot second, is important. Right-left tends to shift the majority of weight to the left. Left-right tends to place the majority of the weight on the right (which is correct).

5. Note that your shoulders are parallel to the flight line.

ADDRESS

Having aligned yourself, you are at the ball, taking your address position.

Illustration 8
Address Position
  • **Align body so that
     shoulders, hips, knees,
     feet are all on lines
     parallel to target line**
  • **Straighten spine**
  • **Keep chin up**
  • **Bend from hips**
  • **Flex knees**
  • **Sit slightly, buttocks out**
  • **Extend arms**
  • **Relax**

Begin by straightening your spine! The spine is the focal point—the axis—around which the body turns away from the target and back to face the target. If your spine is "bent," there will be problems and adjustments to be made. Set it straight and keep it straight!

Basically, your shoulders, hips, and toes are parallel to the flight line and the ball is positioned on the flight line, between your spine and left shoulder.

Applying the following ten *Address Absolutes* will assure correct performance every time.

ADDRESS ABSOLUTES

1. **Bend from your hips**	To keep spine straight
2. **Sit slightly, buttocks out**	For balance
3. **Flex knees**	For lower-body "spring" on *Turnthrough*
4. **Chin up**	Helps straighten spine
5. **Set head position**	To keep head from moving back or down before impact
6. **Position your head approximately one head width behind the ball**	Creates correct "behind-the-ball" position and feeling
7. **Extend your left arm**	A guide through the *Golf Movement*
8. **Relax wrists**	To allow unrestricted cocking and uncocking
9. **Breathe with diaphragm**	Helps relax body
10. **Exhale, begin *Turnback***	Exhale relaxes; inhale tightens

Practice this ten-step process until it becomes a routine performance of one or two seconds, like a reflex. When you are comfortable with these *Address Absolutes,* you are ready for Chapter 3, *The Golf Movement.*

Summary

A correct grip is essential to keep the club face square to the flight line through the impact zone.

The principal function of the address position is to prepare your body to perform the *Golf Movement.*

The sequence for establishing the address position is club head, left foot, right foot.

The straight spine, established at address, is the axis around which your body can turn backward, then forward.

There are ten *Address Absolutes* to be performed routinely, without thought, for all standard shots.

Chapter 3

THE GOLF MOVEMENT
Turnback, Transition, Turnthrough

The information in this chapter applies to all standard shots, regardless of the club used.

The correct *Golf Movement* has three stages: *Turnback, Transition,* and *Turnthrough.* Learning the *Golf Movement* is like learning to tie your shoes or ride a bicycle. Once you learn it, you neither forget nor lose the know-how.

For the very low handicapper, accomplishing the *Golf Movement* may mean learning only one or two new techniques. For the high handicapper, the turning-turning concept may be like learning an entirely new golf game. In either case, the knowledge and skills acquired will allow you to play consistent and correct golf shots—every time, for as many years as you play golf.

RELAX

Relaxation is the cornerstone of the *Golf Movement.*

It seems simple, but remaining relaxed during the entire shot is much more difficult in golf than in any other sport. There are two reasons for this: (1) lack of continuous, vigorous movement and (2) an extended time frame. In other sports, rapid movement and a split-second time frame for making shots leaves little time for physical tension to develop.

There are actions, however, you can take that will aid relaxation during your shot making. Each of these actions shares one word—continuous. Waggle the club, look up at the hole, breathe deeply, move your feet up and down—it doesn't matter as long as the moves are unhurried, smooth, and continuous.

An excellent aid to the relaxation process is to make a complete *Golf Movement,* "a rehearsal," away from the ball. As well as providing continuous movement, this has the added feature of repetition. For the two or three seconds between your rehearsal and the actual shot, you will mentally retain this practiced action, greatly increasing your chances of accurately repeating it when you make the shot.

While you are learning, ask yourself after each shot: "Did I remain relaxed during the full performance of the *Golf Movement*?"

A relaxed body and a calm mind create the canvas upon which the *Golf Movement* is painted.

THE TURNBACK

The *Turnback* begins when your body mass and *Unit* simultaneously turn away from the address position. Keep in mind (from Exercise 3) that your body's turning *causes* your *Unit* to move. Don't start with your arms. Your *Unit* and body start back together.

At that moment, the golf-club head begins tracking on

an imaginary inclined plane that extends from the ball through your shoulders.

Your entire body mass turns away from the ball.

Your shoulders are the "hinge" for the *Golf Movement,* the one connecting point between your body mass and *Unit.* Like all hinges, they move smoothly and freely. Don't tighten your shoulders in an effort to generate power.

Illustration 9: The Turnback

- The turning body has started the club on its backward-upward path
- Both arms are extended
- Both knees are flexed
- Right hip is inside of outer edge of right shoe

- Hips are approaching 45° and shoulders 90° from flight line
- Majority of weight is on right side
- Head is one head width behind the ball position

Your *Unit,* relaxed and passive, directs the golf club on a backward and upward track. As the golf club continues upward, your wrists begin to cock. The weight of the golf club naturally causes this. Your wrists are fully cocked when your *Unit* has brought the golf club to its apex.

There are three faults frequently seen in the play of those who have not mastered this technique:

1. The first is seen in the golfer who believes that power will come from his arms and hands and wants to move his arms independently. He is a product of "the great illusion."

The golfer who is learning to play correctly is seriously misled when he sees a professional, in person or on television, performing the *Golf Movement.* The overall impression is that the arms alone are producing the golf shot. The movement of the arms, hands, and club is so visually dominant that the spectator believes that this alone is responsible for the shot. It is not difficult to see why he then joins the vast majority of amateur golfers who swing the club back with their arms and hands.

2. The second fault is the ruinous "flying right elbow." Miller Barber, Jack Nicklaus, and Uncle Charlie notwithstanding, the right elbow must stay close to the body through the *Golf Movement.*

The "flying right elbow" is usually the result of an arms-dominant swing. Free-swinging arms become random. Without turning-body guidance, the right-arm momentum causes it to move, unchecked, upward and away from the body. The right arm is flailing. The club head is well off its plane. The shot is ruined.

This error is rarely self-detected. Professional assistance or a video aid is required to effect its cure.

3. The third fault occurs when the golfer br.. club back on a path inside the established plane in an effort to later hit from "inside to outside." You learned in the exercises that the correct club-head path is "inside to inside" and that taking the club head off its plane and out of its required orbit spells disaster. If you take the club directly inside the plane, the moment your body begins the *Turnthrough,* your shoulders are forced to "cast" the club outside. At that moment, the *Turnthrough* is destroyed. Your hands have been forced outside of their correct downward path and spend the rest of the shot trying to recover, which they cannot do. Start the club head back on the swing plane and it will arrive where it should be, when it should be there.

After you complete the *Turnback,* think about what has happened and note your position.

The natural turning action of your body mass and *Unit* together has moved 70 to 80 percent of your body weight to the right. Your shoulders have turned about 90 degrees, your hips about half of that. Your back is to the target. This enhances the feeling of being "behind" rather than "over" the ball. Your right leg is flexed, your knee bent, so you are in a position to drive forward and upward on the *Turnthrough.* The outside of your right leg is inside the outer edge of your right shoe.

CONCLUSION

All actions have contributed to being behind the ball. There has been a relaxed and unhurried preparation, a strong sense of being "set."

Illustration 10: The Turnback/Transition

The *Turnback* is a turning action that is deliberate and unhurried but purposeful. There is a strong sense of "winding up." Examples of winding up or "getting set" can be seen in many forms. The professional tennis player prepares to hit a powerful backhand shot. He winds up by turning his lead shoulder well back and under. His wrist is fully cocked.

Some golf instructors refer to the *Turnback* as a "coiling." If you like this description, think of a snake coiled and ready to strike.

A classic example of "set-release" or "prepare-strike" is a cat's position before it springs at its prey. The cat may still be moving forward, but its body lowers and its ears come back—a reflex action. Some muscles contract while others relax and stretch. Finally, the last signal: The tail begins to twitch. He is ready.

There is one significant difference between the set-release of the cat, snake, or tennis player and that of the golfer. For them, the set and release are two distinct acts. *One is completed before the other begins.* Not so with the golfer. The body and *Unit* don't complete the *Turnback* together and then begin the *Turnthrough* together. Rather, the golfer has reached the critical point of *Transition,* the action that creates and stores power used in accelerating through the point of impact.

THE TRANSITION

During the *Turnback,* when your body has reached the point from which it will reverse direction, your *Unit* is still *going up.* This signals the beginning of the *Transition.*

Take a moment to imagine this action. Your turning body has a shorter distance to go than the club head so your body's part of the *Turnback* is completed while your *Unit* is still moving upward. Your body has only two choices: It can wait for your *Unit* to "catch up" or it can begin the *Turnthrough.* It chooses the latter—always.

Your hips make a distinct torque or twisting action to the left; *your feet and legs are a definite part of this move.* Your left leg extends to form a brace but is not stiff or rigid. Your lower body seems to be telling your *Unit,* "Aha! I've got you now. You have to continue going up, but I'm ready to turn—and I'm going to do just that."

THE CONTRA

There is one move that almost every successful PGA Tour player makes. Conversely, this move is all but unknown to amateur golfers. This feature is a significant factor in golf-shot direction and is a major source of power: It is delayed wrist uncocking.

This is the *Contra*—the movement that occurs when the *Unit* and the lower body are simultaneously moving in *opposite* directions.

Illustration 11: Transition/Contra

Transition	*Contra*
• *Unit* slows to its apex	• Left heel is down
• Majority of the body mass is on the right side	• Left knee has moved to the target
• Left shoulder is under the chin	• Hips have started to turn
• Left arm is fully extended	• *Club head is in the same location as in left illustration*
• Wrists are cocked	
• Left heel is up slightly	

You already know that the *Unit,* guided by your extended left arm, will have directed the club back along the orbit path to go backward and upward. With your wrists relaxed, there will come a time when the club's weight causes your wrists to start cocking. This will only occur if the grip is light but sensitive.

This is the signal.

Between this movement and that which occurs when the fully cocked wrists reach their apex, your lower body begins its counterclockwise turn—the *Contra.* You should not think of it as an exact or precise instance.

Using any golf club, practice this move in a relaxed, leisurely manner until you have a sense of the *Contra* movement. As you become adept at this exercise, you will notice that when your wrists cock, your turning left hip becomes a reflex action.

It should now be apparent why, earlier in the book, so much emphasis was placed on body mass (not your shoulders and arms) taking the club back.

If your shoulders and arms take the club back, both the golf club and your body reach their change-of-direction position at the same time. From this position, it is no longer possible to move simultaneously in opposite directions as required for performance of the *Contra* movement.

CONCLUSION

The lower body has initiated the **Turnthrough** while the club head is still in its apex position.

The active lower body is in control. The upper body is passive.

The **Contra** is subtle—but sure.

Few golfers can afford to give up the increase in distance of 12 to 20 percent guaranteed by the effortless *Contra* movement.

Correctly executed, the *Contra* causes seven good things to happen automatically.

"THE MAGNIFICENT SEVEN"

1. The **Unit** coasts to its apex because your turning body, its impetus, has changed direction.
2. The arms-and-hands "hit instinct" disappears when you become aware that your lower body is going to **lead through**.
3. Your lower-body torque "clears out," encouraging an inside-to-inside stroke.
4. Your turning right hip forces the club to stay on the same, and correct, downward plane.
5. Your lower body has time to "get set and on balance" before the arms and club arrive, therefore delivering maximum power from the legs.
6. There is no effort to hurry or "cast" the club at the ball, so your wrists remain cocked longer, producing more club-head speed at impact and, thus, greater distance.
7. At impact there is a strong and true sense of being "behind the ball."

A frequently overlooked phenomenon relates directly to the *Contra* movement. Most amateurs in the 5 to 15 handicap range hit nearly the same distance with their number 7, number 8, and number 9 irons as the scratch amateurs and professionals. Not the same but close. As the shots get longer, this near parity changes dramatically. For the number 2 and number 3 iron and driver shots, the difference in distance is significantly greater. Why?

On short-iron shots, the arms-hands hit used by most amateurs has enough force to send the ball the required distance; on longer shots, this hit proves glaringly inadequate.

The professional uses the *Contra* to initiate lower-body torque—a power source. The amateur has never been shown what the *Contra* is.

THE TURNTHROUGH

The *Transition* is over. The *Unit* goes from passive to active. Concurrently, you are in the middle of the *Turnthrough* and this is what has happened.

Your left hip, turning to the left, has initiated the *Turnthrough.* Consequently, some of the weight that was on the right shifts to the left. The speed and forceful turning of your hips causes your arms to move downward, bringing your hands (wrists fully cocked) to a position approximately opposite your waist. Your extended left leg and hip have formed a brace to allow your right hip to drive through and up. *This very important move prevents your hips from sliding past the ball position and keeps the majority of your weight on the right side at impact.* This is a "reverse corkscrew" for the left leg and hip: *counterclockwise and up.*

Most PGA Tour professionals have their left hip behind the outside of their left foot at impact. Arnold Palmer has a bent left leg but twists his hips forcefully to keep them from sliding forward and past the ball position. "Violent" is the only word for the forward movement Chi Chi Rodriguez makes on his tee shots; but if you look closely you will see his extended left leg is set behind the ball position. For yourself, make sure your left-hip torque is accompanied by an extended left leg.

Illustration 12: The Turnthrough

1. At the *Turnback* apex, the wrists are fully cocked and the hips are 45° from the target line.

2. Hands are opposite the waist. Wrists are still fully cocked. Hips have turned past the target line.

3. At impact, the lower body faces the target. The head and majority of body mass remain behind the ball position.

<—Note: Ball is gone. Right hand has not turned over.

CONCLUSION

The lower body is *active* and the upper body is passive.
The lower body *pulls* the upper body on the **Turnthrough.**
The lower body does this with a *smoothly accelerating torque* action.

You are at the moment of truth in the golf shot—that moment when the "good-hit instinct" takes over. The good-hit instinct occurs when your hands/wrists (passive from the beginning) become active. In fact, if you have performed the *Golf Movement* properly to this point, it is impossible to stop your hands/wrists from becoming active. With a crack-the-whip action, they drive the club head with great velocity through the ball position.

NOTE
If your arms, wrists, and hands were active before, they are now unable to perform this critical function.

At this moment, direction and distance are determined.

DIRECTION

The position of the club face immediately prior to, during, and just after impact determines direction.

Your extended left arm, your early-turning lower body forcing the golf club to take the correct downward path, your stable feet, spine/axis, and head . . . all ensure that as the club head approaches the ball it is square to the target line and remains so through impact.

At impact, your right hand is in just the same position it was at address. It remains in this position through impact and beyond (see Illustration 12, number 3, and Illustration 13).

DISTANCE

"Wait a minute," you say. "How can I get power if I don't roll my wrists? Anyway, once my wrists are uncocking they just naturally pronate. How can I get power otherwise?"

Maximum power is generated when club-head velocity, created by your unlocking wrists, is increased by the torquing action of your upper body. Your feet, spine/axis, and head are in place. Your left leg has extended to form a brace.

In contrast, the club head is accelerating as it approaches the ball. Your lower body is continuing to turn toward the target. But now your upper body is turning faster than your lower body. (This is clearly shown in Illustration 12, in which the lower body has turned further counterclockwise than the upper, and in Illustration 13, in which the upper body has turned further than the lower, i.e., through the hitting area, the upper body was turning faster.)

Again, upper-body torque and uncocking wrists, occurring simultaneously, is what produces the maximum impact force of the club head meeting the golf ball.

If you are an amateur golfer, this may come to you as a revelation: If the right hand does *not* pronate through impact, you will achieve maximum distance.

Go to your practice area. Start with pitch shots and short irons. With patience, you will see positive results. Stick with it. Work up to longer shots. When you hit woods and then your driver, you will find that what we said is correct.

Your drives will be consistently longer and your accuracy will have increased as well.

THE FINISH

The "follow-through" is the final action of the *Golf Movement*. The club head strikes the ball and, just past impact, reaches its maximum speed. From this point, everything decelerates and you enter the final stage.

It would be incorrect to say, "The follow-through is automatic and therefore unimportant." An incomplete or faulty finish signals a bad shot. If you ignore the mistake(s) made at the finish and repeat them, you will repeat bad shots.

For example: Having your weight hang back and remain on the right side after striking the ball produces a poor finish. Having your hands (and club) go low and to the left after striking the ball is another bad finish.

The following checkpoints will confirm a correct follow-through.

A. Be sure your extended right arm continues on the swing plane after impact. In the same way your extended left arm was a guide for your *Unit* on the *Turnback* and to club impact, your extended right arm is the guide as the club head approaches the ball and continues past impact. Both arms are extended for the first time since the address position. Watch the very best golfers exhibit the extended right arm after impact for all the regular shots.

Illustration 13: The Finish
The right arm remains extended well into the finish.

  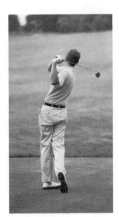

- The left hip has turned more than 90° from the target line.
- The left shoulder has turned back farther than the left hip.

CONCLUSION

There is a signature when the three finish checkpoints are all correctly performed—perfect balance.

B.   The position of your left hip and shoulder at the finish will verify correct performance of the ***Turn-through.*** As you pose briefly, on balance, your left hip will have turned 90 degrees or more from the ball's flight line; your shoulders will have turned even further. Your left shoulder will have turned past your left hip at the finish. It is physically impossible to attain this correct finish if a player has allowed his hips to slide past the ball position or has not kept the majority of his weight behind the ball at impact.

On the follow-through, be sure to pay attention to these three checkpoints: the right arm extension, the final position of the left hip, and the final position of the left shoulder.

You have now learned the correct and complete *Golf Movement.* With practice and experience, you will appreciate the following quote and, in time, you will "get your swing grooved" too.

Wayne Levi [on the PGA Tour] was quoted by USA Today, *August 23, 1990, as follows:*

"Once you get your swing grooved, you don't have to work on it. Those guys who pound balls, tinker with their swings all the time are doing something wrong . . . All I have to do when I get to a tournament is stretch my muscles."

This, from a man who won four PGA Tour tournaments and over a million dollars in 1990 and was voted PGA Tour Player of the Year.

There will be days when you don't play well. At these times, look to the mental aspects of your round: Did you bring a mentally stressful situation to the course? Did things happen during play that upset you? Were you physically or mentally weary before you began?

Before you ever make a physical change in a *Golf Movement* that is correct and has served you well, consider these mental forces at work and:

Don't Tinker

SUMMARY

The *Golf Movement* is the same for all standard golf shots: chip shots, pitch shots, bunker shots, short irons, long irons, fairway woods, and tee shots. The only difference is quantitative.

The *Golf Movement Absolutes* are performed within an invisible cylinder whose sides rise from just outside your right and left foot to waist height.

Your body and *Unit* together initiate the *Turnback.*

Your active turning body swings the passive *Unit.*

The club weight alone creates the wrist cock.

Your body completes its *Turnback* before your *Unit* arrives at its apex.

Your body begins the *Turnthrough* while your *Unit* is still going up. This is the *Transition* stage and contains the *Contra.*

A counterclockwise and upward move of your left hip and leg establishes a brace.

Your turning hips cause your *Unit* to lower.

As your passive *Unit* brings your hands to an area

about opposite your waist, your *Unit* becomes active, your wrists uncock.

At impact, 55 to 65 percent of your weight is on the right side (behind the ball).

In an on-balance finish, your hips and shoulders have turned more than 90 degrees from the target line; you are directly facing the target.

Accuracy is achieved by your turning and leading body, making your *Unit* follow the same path on each shot.

Distance is initiated by lower-body turning. Delayed wrist uncocking and upper-body torque occurring simultaneously produces maximum force at impact.

The *Turnback, Transition,* and *Turnthrough* are the complete *Golf Movement.*

When you have learned the correct *Golf Movement* . . .

Don't Tinker

PROGRESSION CHART
GOLF SHOTS

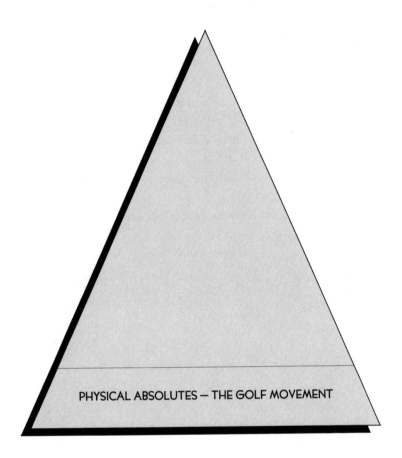

PHYSICAL ABSOLUTES — THE GOLF MOVEMENT

Chapter 4

GREENSIDE
PLAY

Chipping and pitching are basically the same stroke. They differ only in the distance the ball travels and the club used. The standard chip and pitch shots will be discussed here. Chapter 6 will address special short-game shots.

The chip and pitch shots are a miniaturized version of the full *Golf Movement.* The preshot routine is the same; the preshot address and *Movement Absolutes* are the same. The essential difference between a chip/pitch shot and a full golf shot is quantitative rather than qualitative.

For a greenside shot, your body need only move slightly to swing the *Unit* back. As your body turns gently toward the target, this move, and gravity, are sufficient to send the club head through the ball position with enough force to cause the ball to get to its target.

There are five *Absolutes* associated with your short shots. The first of these is grip pressure. These are "feel-and-touch" shots. They will be successful when made with a light grip pressure that never increases during the stroke. Imagine your hands on a car steering wheel or a bird held in your hands. The grip pressure is gentle but secure.

The second *Absolute* is pace or tempo. The back tempo is slower than the forward. When the ball is close to the hole, there is a strong, natural tendency to "help the shot" by using your hands. Resist this by making a mini-*Movement* with a good tempo, and allow gravity to cause the club head to strike the ball.

The third *Absolute* is line-angle-line. At address, regardless of the ball's position in relation to the feet, your left arm and golf club form a near straight line. When you make the shot, the club shaft forms an angle with your left arm on the backward path. When the club makes its forward movement, it returns to the left-arm-club straight line at impact.

The fourth *Absolute* is the extension of your left leg at impact. To achieve this, begin your forward movement, the *Turnthrough,* by extending your left leg—this is a counterclockwise and upward movement of your left hip. This allows your right hip and then the golf club to move freely to the target. A pronounced open stance makes this performance much easier and is strongly recommended.

The fifth *Absolute* is having your body face the target as you watch the ball roll into the hole.

Again, the final word is that the chip/pitch shot is simply a miniaturized version of the full golf shot.

Once you understand and accept these *Absolutes* as essential for consistent greenside play, variations can be more comfortably explored.

The following variations determine the distance and/or the trajectory of the shot:

Club selection
Ball position and shaft-to-ground angle at address
Length of stroke back

Variation #1

Club selection

The pitch, or "lob" shot, requires maximum air time and minimum ground roll. Play this shot with the sand wedge. For shots over a hazard where there is considerable distance on the green from the hazard to the hole, a pitching wedge may be a better choice.

For short air time and long ground roll, you can chip successfully with a number of different clubs. This choice will depend on the amount of time you use for practice and play.

If you spend twenty-five hours or more per week (at least ten of which are spent practicing) on your golf, then you can learn to play all the clubs from the number 5 iron through the pitching wedge. If your golfing time is confined to two rounds per week and no more than two or three hours of practice, it would be prudent to limit your chipping to two clubs: a number 7 iron and a pitching wedge. This will eliminate decision making and uncertainty. If your chip shot requires a long roll, you select your "good ol' trusty" number 7 iron. If the rolling distance is short, you use your "good ol' reliable" pitching wedge—no decisions, no uncertainty, no negatives.

Variation #2

Ball position and shaft-to-ground angle at address

There are three basic positions:

1. *Ball back, shaft forward.* This produces a low running shot. Play this with your number 7 iron or pitching wedge.

2. *Ball centered, shaft centered.* This shot covers about equal distance in the air and on the ground. Play this with a sand wedge or a pitching wedge.

Illustration 14

The exact same stroke produces all three shots.

The ball's position determines the shaft's angle at address and impact.

Ball back, shaft forward—produces low running shot.

Ball centered, shaft centered—produces equal air and ground distance.

Ball forward, shaft back—produces a lob shot with maximum air and minimum ground time.

3. *Ball forward, shaft back.* This creates the lob shot, maximum air time, and minimum ground time. Play this only with a sand wedge.

Variation #3

Length of stroke back

Once you select the club and establish the ball position and shaft-to-ground angle, you need only decide how far to take the club back.

MYTHS

Over the years, myths have developed around the short shots.

Myth #1: "Keep your head down."

On putts, yes. On short shots, NO! Allow your head to rotate so your eyes never lose sight of the ball from the instant of impact until the ball stops rolling.

Myth #2: "Stay still—don't move."

Again, okay on putts, but on short shots definitely NO! These shots are delicate and when done correctly are characterized by physical fluidity. If you program your mind to "stay still," you will never be able to play these shots with consistent skill and accuracy.

Myth #3: "Keep your wrists stiff."

Stiff wrists remove all feel and frequently produce a jab or push stroke that becomes more prevalent as the importance of the shot increases.

If you believe even one of these myths, it will be very destructive to your short game.

Use your eyes, use your body, use your wrists. Your instincts will teach you to play these shots successfully.

Imagine you are sitting on the porch of the golf clubhouse and a foursome of amateurs is approaching the green in front of you. This is a long par 4 and all of the players are short of the green. One is in a greenside bunker and the other three are on the fairway some 100, 30, and 6 feet from the green. You are about 100 yards away. It is easy to visualize each shot they will play. As the amateurs make their shots, they become mirror images of one another. Each is a complete arms/hands hit at the ball with no correct body movement. The sand shot is "dug" and barely reaches the green. The longest approach is hit thin and goes off line and long. The second is hit "fat." The final shot goes onto the green but well off line.

The second act of this scene stars two professionals and two very low handicap golfers. Since they played the long tees, their balls are in approximately the same positions as those in the previous group. Each player, in turn, makes his shot and every one is a miniature version of the *Golf Movement.* The body turns in one direction and then back. Since the distance the ball is to be propelled is short, the club seems to free-fall from its apex. You see that each shot seems lazy. In every case the ball lands softly on the green and rolls as planned toward its target. Each player in this group has learned that there is one *Golf Movement.* Chip, pitch, sand, short irons, long irons, and drivers are all played with the same *Turnback, Turnthrough* motion.

The players in the first foursome were trying to make the shot happen. Those in the second group were "set on automatic." They *let* the shot happen.

Once you accept, learn, and use this knowledge, your golf game will be much easier—and thus more enjoyable.

SUMMARY

There are five *Absolutes* for greenside play:

1. Maintain a light grip pressure that never increases
2. Maintain stroke tempo
3. Remember: Line-angle-line of the left arm and club
4. Move left hip and leg counterclockwise and upward
5. Watch the ball from impact into the hole

Three variations determine the distance and trajectory of the shot:

1. Club selection
2. Ball position and shaft-to-ground angle at address
3. Length of stroke back

There are three myths to be expelled from your greenside play:

1. Keep your head down
2. Stay still—don't move
3. Keep your wrists stiff

Chip and pitch shots are gentle, abbreviated versions of the *Golf Movement.*

Chapter 5

SAND PLAY

Your golf ball is on the fairway some 170 yards from the green. One of your playing companions is a professional whose ball is also on the fairway. As he has played the back tees, his ball is the same distance from the hole as yours. This green has sand traps on both sides that curve around the front to catch a shot that is short and either right or left. Over the green is thick rough.

As you look at your shot, you think, "Boy, that's a lotta sand—right, left, short. I really hate getting in sand traps. I never know how the ball will come out—if it does."

The professional looks at his shot and thinks, "Where is the pin?" He never gives the bunkers a second thought. He knows if he hits an errant shot into the sand he will come out close enough to have a good chance to make the putt.

One of the shots the professional regards as the easiest, the amateur finds frightening and difficult. This is rather like the pilot who knows aerodynamics—what causes lift and thrust. He knows he can land a four-engine plane with only one engine working. A pilot knows he can glide a plane, with no engine power, to a landing. Compare this to the person who has a fear of the heavy plane dropping from the sky.

The difference is really one word: knowledge. Once you gain the knowledge the professional has, then practice to confirm this knowledge, there is no reason in the world why you cannot become a consistently good bunker player. You'll replace uncertainty and fear with confidence.

There are five characteristics of the standard sand shot. The first of these is the most important, but it is also the one you are the least likely to know . . . or at least believe.

1. For standard sand shots, use exactly the same *Golf Movement* you employ for your regular shots. That's the key, and isn't it nice that you don't have anything new to learn?

2. Use an open stance and position the ball opposite your left heel. Open the club face.

3. Squirm your feet into the sand to establish good balance so that during the shot your feet will not slide.

4. Make your normal *Golf Movement* and slide the club face under the ball. Because the sand-wedge angle is built to accomplish this, the ball will rise into the air and arc gently onto the green.

5. Don't scoop! Don't dig! Don't lift! Don't push! Don't help! The normal *Golf Movement* will accomplish the desired result. Trust and confidence will replace fear and uncertainty.

Amateur golfers almost always would rather play a shot from the rough than from the sand. Once you have learned how to execute the shot, it will become clear why the professional prefers a shot from the sand rather than from the rough.

There is greater margin for error from the sand than

from the rough. A sand shot made where the wedge does not enter precisely where you aimed will still cause the ball to stop on the green. Such a mis-hit from the rough likely will not.

Ball reaction out of the sand is predictable and therefore controllable. Out of the rough it is not.

Out of the sand you can make the ball stop quickly, even though the air time is long. This is impossible out of the rough.

It's very likely the day may come when you prefer to play from the sand rather than from the rough.

ALTERED SAND SHOTS

Beyond the basic shot played from a greenside bunker, there are a number of altered sand shots. Almost all of these are ball position and/or club-to-ground angle adjustments *made at address*. After that, you simply use your *Golf Movement*.

1. **Fairway Bunker**
   Establish very solid footing
   Hit the ball before the sand
   Use the next longer club
                         BALL ACTION: Normal Roll

2. **Long Greenside Bunker**
   Shot requires 30- to 50-foot carry over sand
   Move ball back in stance
   Square up, or slightly close, club face
   Make full swing, hitting sand first
                         BALL ACTION: Short Roll

3. Hard Sand, Greenside

Open the club face
Hit under ball; no ball contact
>BALL ACTION: Long Roll

4. Wet Sand, Greenside

Wet sand is heavy and will slow club head
Close club face
Play ball in the middle of the stance
>BALL ACTION: Medium Roll

5. Flat Bunker at Green Level

Ball close to green; no, or low, lip
Use number 7, 8, or 9 iron, depending on distance
  required
Keep body still; use putting stroke
Use either regular or putting grip
Hit ball first
>BALL ACTION: Ball Rolls Like Putt

6. Uphill Beside Green

Dig in feet
Put maximum weight on left side
Set shoulders parallel to angle of the slope
>BALL ACTION: Short Roll

7. Ball Buried in Bunker Face

Dig feet in securely
Align hips and shoulders to angle of the slope
>BALL ACTION: Long Roll

8. Downhill, Greenside
Play ball off right foot
Put shaft forward
Align hips and knees to slope
Plan for ball to roll far
> BALL ACTION: Long Roll

9. Sidehill: Ball Above Feet
Play ball off right foot
Close club face
Hit under ball; no ball contact
Make full swing
> BALL ACTION: Long and Right-to-left Roll

10. Sidehill: Ball Below Feet
Dig feet in deeply
Bend both knees—sit-down posture
Use open stance and aim left of hole
> BALL ACTION: Long and Left-to-right Roll

11. Buried Ball: Greenside
Close club face
Let gravity create club-head speed
Ball pops out with "dead" or "splash" effect
Don't force, or help, the shot
> BALL ACTION: Short Roll

As with all golf shots, proficiency comes with practice. The first step is to develop skill and confidence with the basic sand shot. Once you have done this, plan to learn the variations in groups in which the shots have similar characteristics. Fairway and long greenside bunker shots should be learned together. Uphill, downhill, and sidehill shots should be practiced as a group. Buried balls in the floor or face of a bunker require similar shots.

The quality of your practice, not the duration, is important. Plan your practice session and follow your plan. These sand shots will soon become a standard and comfortable part of your golf game.

SUMMARY

For standard sand shots, make your *Golf Movement.* Have the club head enter the sand behind, and pass under, the ball. This will force the ball into the air and onto the green.

Don't scoop! Don't dig! Don't lift! Don't push! Don't help!

Altered sand shots require adjustments dictated by the ball's position in the sand. Each of these must be individually learned.

Objectively, sand shots are not difficult to play. As with all your shots, it is simply a matter of replacing uncertainty and fear with knowledge. Knowledge, fortified through practice and experience, becomes confidence. A confident sand player is a good sand player.

Chapter 6

ALTERED SHOTS

These are usually called special shots, but special implies "unique," "extraordinary," "exceptional." The golf shots described here are not so; they are simply regular golf shots in which an adjustment, usually slight, has been made to accommodate the ball's position.

The large majority of these shots are made by a single adjustment at the address position. In a few cases, wrist action is altered. After you make the required change, use the *Golf Movement* to perform the shot. Don't try to "help" the shot by some additional physical action during the stroke.

The situations described below will use one or more of the following to make the altered shots:

Club changed
Posture changed
Ball position moved
Club-to-ground angle altered
Target changed
Wrist action altered

1. Ball is adjacent to the green, but in the short rough. Or in the first cut, but in a depression. Or, it is on the green, but against the collar.

>**ALTER: Club change**
>>Use a sand wedge and have the leading edge strike the center of the ball
>>
>>Use your putting stroke
>
>**RESULT:** Wedge sole pushes down the grass so the club's leading edge strikes the ball cleanly and it rolls like a putt.

2. Ball is in a divot, either in the fairway or rough.

>**ALTER: Club change; ball position; club-to-ground angle**
>>Use one more lofted club
>>
>>Move the ball back in the stance
>>
>>Have hands centered so club-to-ground angle changes
>>
>>Make normal *Golf Movement,* striking the ball first
>
>**RESULT:** Ball will come out low and running.

3. Full shot in which ball is on bare, hard ground, on pine needles, leaves, or other potential encumbrance.

>**ALTER: Ball position, club-to-ground angle**
>>Move the ball back in the stance
>>
>>Have hands centered so club-to-ground angle changes
>>
>>Strike ball first ("trap it" or "pinch it")
>
>**RESULT:** Ball lands with one bounce and short roll.

4. Playing shots into the wind.
   ALTER: Club change, ball position, club-to-ground angle
   > Use one or two longer clubs
   > Move the ball back in the stance
   > Have hands centered so club-to-ground angle changes
   > Make normal *Golf Movement*

   RESULT: Ball flight is low, straight, and strong with no forward roll; carry ball to target (a "knockdown" shot).

5. Playing downwind shots.
   ALTER: Club change
   > Take one or two less clubs

   RESULT: Play for a long roll when ball lands, due to the wind taking spin off the ball.

6. Uphill lie.
   ALTER: Alter the target
   > Ball in middle of stance
   > Aim to the right of the target
   > Align hips and shoulders parallel to the ground slope
   > Weight on right side
   > Balance is critical; use shorter and easier stroke

   RESULT: Natural ball flight is a draw.

7. Downhill lie.
   ALTER: Alter the target
   > Aim to the left of the target

Align hips and shoulders parallel to the ground
   slope
Weight on left side
Balance is critical; use shorter and easier stroke
RESULT: Natural ball flight is a fade.

8. Sidehill, ball above feet.
   Same as 6

9. Sidehill lie, ball below feet.
   Same as 7

10. Ball in the rough, near or adjacent to the green.
    **ALTER: Ball position, club-to-ground angle, wrist
    action**
      Play the ball off the left foot
      Center the hands
      Open the club face
      Have relaxed wrists/soft hands
      At impact, club shaft and arms have returned to
         the address position.
    RESULT: Ball has high arc and short roll.

11. Shaped shot: a fade.
    ALTER: Feet, hip, and shoulder alignment
      Aim club face at the target
      Aim feet, hips, and shoulders left of the target
      The club's path is along the body's alignment
      Use your normal *Golf Movement*
    RESULT: Ball has a high arc and little roll. Ball's
    flight is left to right, a fade.

12. Shaped shot: a draw.
   ALTER: Feet, hip, and shoulder alignment
      Aim club face at the target
      Aim feet, hips, and shoulders right of the target
      The club's path is along the body's alignment
      Use your normal *Golf Movement*
   RESULT: Ball flight is right to left, a draw.

The only way to play altered shots consistently well is to practice them regularly. If your first reaction is that these occur so infrequently that it's not worth the trouble, consider this: Altered shots are required because the ball has come to rest in a position other than a flat lie in the fairway. You may have read what to do, but do you remember? When you are confronted with these shots without having practiced them regularly, the thought of the adjustments that must be made will certainly produce a bad shot—count on it. Further, bad shots from bad ball positions frequently create a double jeopardy. The ball has gone from a bad to a worse position. This creates strong negative emotions.

Examples of this are many. You find your ball in a downhill lie in the rough above the green. There is a sand trap between the ball and the green. If you hit short, you're in the sand. A too long shot will put you in the rough or another trap. Another example: Your ball has come to rest in the high rough beside the green. The ball is only fifteen feet from the hole. Not knowing what to do, you try to hit a gentle shot. The high grass entwines the hosel of your club and the ball stays in the rough. Determined to get the ball free, you hit it harder and skull it over the green. The litany goes on.

Succinctly, an inability to play altered shots correctly will almost certainly cause one or both of the following:

More than just one shot will be added on that particular hole.

Negative emotions will be generated. These will be retained and produce additional bad shots on subsequent holes.

Conversely, playing the bad-ball position shots correctly will add no more than one shot to your score. There is the real possibility that your good play will "save a shot."

There is nothing that will be a greater stimulus to creating a positive attitude than a skillfully played recovery shot.

For a lower score and a sustained positive attitude, you must make these shots an integral part of your game. Accomplish this by practicing until altered shots become standard shots.

SUMMARY

To play altered shots, you must change one or more of the following:

> Your club selection
> Your posture
> The ball position at address
> The club-to-ground angle
> The target
> Your wrist action

Playing altered shots well lowers your score. It also keeps negative emotions out and creates a positive attitude.

Chapter 7

ROUTINE, PRACTICE

ROUTINE

Picture one of the best professional basketball players in the NBA at the free throw line.

First there is the *Variable* stage. He may walk away from the foul line, bounce the ball a number of times, or make a practice motion with his shooting arm. Once he has finished and taken his stance, he moves into the second stage.

The second stage may still contain one or two *Variables,* but it also includes *Absolutes.* He may bounce the ball or glance at the basket *(Variables).* He will breathe deeply, flex his knees, bring the ball to the ready position, and look at the front rim of the basket *(Absolutes).*

The third and final stage is an *Absolute* of movement. The arm moves the ball upward and releases it. With a graceful arc, it tracks end over end, cleanly into the basket.

Hundreds of hours of practice have gone into developing this routine. From the moment it begins until the end, it is a continuous action. It is always the same: He repeats his

Variables and *Absolutes* the same way in the same sequence every time.

What do you think would happen if we said to the foul shooter, "Okay, now we want you to take twenty shots. But you may not use any part of your routine"? You're right. He would think of his new and different physical actions and be lucky if he made half the shots.

You must develop a routine that is as precise and thought-free as that of a world-class foul shooter. Your routine includes any practice moves or actions prior to taking your address position. It includes each move that is part of establishing your address position. Earlier, you learned ten *Absolutes* to perform when taking your stance at the ball. It is imperative that you do them all *in the same sequence every time.*

Your routine will have a rhythm that will be largely determined by your personality. Don't take too long, but don't rush either. Be deliberate, eliminate extraneous movements, and create a sequence you can repeat comfortably. Your goal is to perform your routine with the same thought-free precision you use when tying your shoes.

The following routine is used by many pros, with proven success. It can, of course, be adapted to suit your personal preferences. Remember, simplicity and faithful execution are the keys.

1. Select your club. Stand away from the ball. Perform your address sequence and then make one complete *Golf Movement* of your *Turnback, Transition,* and *Turnthrough.*

2. Approach your ball from behind the ball-to-target flight line. As you do this, look from the ball to the target and visualize the ball's flight.

3. Place the club head behind the ball and then take your stance. Look once again at the target and then back to the ball.

4. Begin your *Golf Movement.*

The procedure outline has been successful because it has built in many positive features and removed negative features:

1. Once begun, the physical action is continuous.

2. The "rehearsal" physically relaxes all your body parts.

3. The rehearsal gives you positive reinforcement for the upcoming shot.

4. By being target-conscious, you eliminate being ball-conscious. Many amateurs come to the golf ball and freeze, making it very difficult to relax and begin their *Golf Movement.*

5. Throughout the routine, all your thoughts are positive. Seeing the path the ball will take to the target is positive; visualizing the ball on that path is positive, and so on.

6. When your mind is filled with positive thoughts, there can be no room for destructive, negative thoughts. This is the principal reason for the necessity of a routine.

DEVELOPING A ROUTINE

A routine can only be developed through constant repetition. Take your full set of clubs to the driving range or practice tee. Select a club and stand away from the ball. Begin your routine, continue through the address position, and finish by hitting the ball. Return the club to the bag, take another, and repeat the procedure. Use all the clubs in your bag and then repeat the sequence several times. The only purpose of these exercises is to develop a routine. Don't get caught up in the results of the golf shot. As you learn your routine, make certain each step is in sequence and completed correctly.

This may not seem to be a challenging or interesting exercise. It is, however, the only way to develop a routine you can repeat time after time without thought. With this accomplished, you are ready to try your routine in action on a practice round of nine holes.

Your only concern for this round should be the correct performance of your routine. Don't keep score or be concerned where the ball goes. If you hit a shot and fail to perform your routine correctly, put down another ball and try again. If there was one part with which you had difficulty, or with which you were uncomfortable, go back to the practice area. Make any modifications, deletions, or additions you think will make your routine better. Return to the course and play another practice round using your new routine. Be prepared to repeat this procedure a number of times. Creating a solid routine is not as easy as it sounds.

The next step is to play eighteen holes, following the same procedure, with your playing partner monitoring your routine.

If you asked a hundred amateurs if they had a routine, the majority would say "Yes" and believe it. In truth, this majority has a general collection of actions they perform at some times and not at others. When an important shot is called for, it is unlikely they employ anything resembling a true routine. Don't be guilty of this. Develop a routine that is definitive, specific, and *the same for all shots.* And then always use it. A true routine is essential. It is a basic requirement for the *Golf Movement.*

PRACTICE

No one would seriously expect to learn to play golf without practicing. No one would expect to improve without practicing. You practice so you can repeat what you have learned—correctly and with consistency.

Make certain that what you are practicing is correct. Practicing what is wrong is like making an automobile trip, taking a wrong turn, and not discovering it until you have gone an hour out of your way. Practicing incorrect technique wastes your time now and later, when the error will have to be unlearned and replaced.

The practice time required will vary with individual abilities and goals. Make a commitment to practice as much as necessary to reach *your* goal.

Plan before reaching the practice area. For example, "Today, I will concentrate only on tempo. I will keep my *Turnback* and *Turnthrough* tempos in mind as I hit all the shots." Whatever it is for that session, make a plan and follow it. Limit the number of specific actions at any one session to a maximum of three. One is preferable.

The practice tee is where you perfect your preshot routine as well as your *Golf Movement*. Make certain each shot you hit includes the complete and correct routine you will use on the golf course. Make each shot a separate and distinct shot. Place your practice balls away from you. Now, before each shot, you must get a ball, bring it to your shooting area, and go through your preshot routine. This action will be encouraged by changing clubs frequently.

There is a strong tendency at practice facilities (because they are so large and wide open) to hit aimless and careless shots. Once you have warmed up, aim each of your shots at a target to further emulate your on-course play.

After missing a shot, there is a temptation to hit the next shot quickly. You know what you did wrong and are anxious to remedy it. Relax. Take it easy. Walk away from your hitting area.

After hitting some fifteen or twenty shots, go and sit down. Have a drink of water. Start over in a calm manner. This will help make your practice session meaningful and productive.

Whenever possible, have someone who knows your "plan for the day" observe what you are doing. More often than not, you will actually be doing something other than what you believe you are doing. Having an objective observer, for at least part of the time, can remedy this.

Get a video camera if you can. There is no single factor as important as a video to give you a clear and accurate picture of exactly what occurred during your practice. This important aid will be addressed at length in the next chapter.

Finally, when you become tired, stop. You'll probably become mentally tired before you become physically tired. Your focus will wander, and you may hit some crazy shots. When this occurs, it is time to quit; any further practice will be counterproductive.

SUMMARY

ROUTINE

Your routine begins after you have decided on the shot you will play, selected your club, and taken it from the bag. You can perform your rehearsal, waggle the club, or go through whatever individual mannerisms constitute your preaddress actions.

Move to the address position and take your stance,

incorporating the *Address Absolutes*—now you are ready to begin the *Golf Movement.*

All that has occurred to this point is your routine. It is a ritual-like performance, individualistic, but the same for all regular golf shots.

Your routine is the foundation for your Golf Movement.

Practice

One of the keys to creating consistency in on-course play is practice. You must do this correctly and with intent.

Your practice has three tenets:

1. Have a plan before arriving at the practice tee. This plan must include a specific time frame and selected shots and goals.

2. Make certain that what you are practicing is correct.

3. Be precise, rather than haphazard, in shot making and target selection.

Finally, the practice area is where you develop your routine. Make certain that each practice shot you hit faithfully includes your preshot routine.

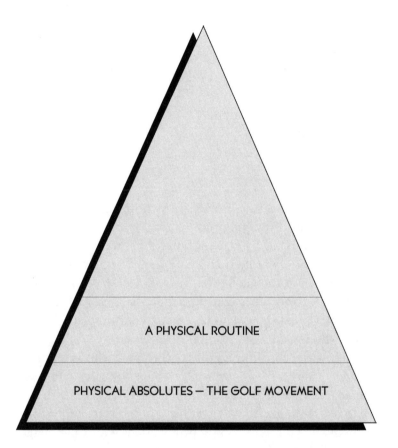

A PHYSICAL ROUTINE

PHYSICAL ABSOLUTES — THE GOLF MOVEMENT

Chapter 8

TEACHING, LEARNING

In the 1940s, the Yale University swimming teams had a string of consecutive victories that still stand as an NCAA record for all sports. The coach, Bob Kiphuth, couldn't swim.

A doctor is a professional, a plumber is a professional, a lawyer is a professional. These three professionals solve your problems for you. They take the action for a resolution. The golf professional shows you how to fix your problem, but it is you who must take the action.

How do you find a golf professional who is a good teacher? Talk to friends who play about the same game as you do and have taken lessons from a particular teacher. If he has helped them, he will certainly be able to help you. Remember, you're seeking a professional who can teach. How well he plays is of no consequence.

WHO ARE YOU?

When you begin with your professional golf teacher, tell him something about yourself. Tell him how often you will play, if you will practice, and how much. Discuss your goals and agree on a reasonable, achievable set; tell him your present problem(s)—sand shots, slice, for instance. In short, talking to him will help him help you.

PLANS

After that, you need a mutually agreed upon plan. First, you should assure him you are not there to take one lesson with the belief that such a "Band-Aid" approach will give you a golf game. Tell him you plan to take as many lessons as required to learn the correct and complete *Golf Movement.* Let him know that even after you have gained this knowledge, you will return periodically for checkups. This removes any time-urgency restraints from his instruction and allows him to do his job.

RESPONSIBILITY

Your goal and his responsibility to teach are the same—complete knowledge and performance of the *Golf Movement* on the practice tee. Your teacher will give you this. Anything more you must do for yourself.

Far too many golf students mistakenly believe that their performance under the instruction of a teacher on the practice tee will automatically be mirrored in their play on the course. If this does not happen, they believe the teacher is somehow at fault for lack of (or wrong) information.

At the practice tee, there are no negatives. There are no

hazards, no rough, no bad lies, no pressure. Bad shots are inconsequential and thus dismissed. In addition, you have the helpful and positive counsel of your instructor.

The course is a different venue. Here you must record every shot. When you are on the golf course, you are alone. Your pro's job is to prepare you for this time. His interest in (and concern for) your future play will go well beyond that. His responsibility, however, is only to teach.

Your challenge will be to translate what you have learned into improved performance on the course.

THE GOLF MOVEMENT

Briefly explain the key concepts in this book and ask him to provide guidance within this framework. Focus on the *Absolutes,* particularly those you have not mastered. Several minutes discussing the *Golf Movement,* the *Turnback, Transition,* and *Turnthrough* will be time well spent.

60-60

Discuss with your professional the 60-60; 60 percent of your shots played are within 60 yards of the hole. To develop a skill in this area is totally independent of such elements as age, sex, size, and strength. With correct initial instruction and diligent practice, you can develop a scratch golf game from 50 to 60 yards into the hole.

Tell your instructor this is one of your specific goals. Work with him to create a plan to accomplish this goal.

PUTTING

Putting is obviously a significant part of the 60-60 plan. After all, the scorecard calls for you to make half your shots on the putting green. You should definitely plan on spending time with your professional on the practice putting green. A missed putt is not only a missed shot—it is unrecoverable.

Good putting brings rewards in the form of fewer strokes. In addition, being a good putter will have a tremendously positive psychological effect on the rest of your game. It will make the difference between missing a shot and saying, "Well, there goes a stroke," and missing a shot and saying, "That's okay. I can make that up on the putting green."

TEE SHOT

There is no question that the most important shot in golf is the tee shot. Sam Snead said it, and it is true. The more difficult the course, the truer this becomes. The top-ranked golf courses are all designed so any errant tee shot is in trouble. From this point on, the golfer is struggling and the results range from a poor hole to disaster. Ask your professional to help you develop one shot that will consistently place your tee shot in play. Discuss the theory that a known trajectory will give you double the fairway target of trying to drive down the middle.

If you can learn to hit the ball from left to right each time, tee up on the far right side of the tee. Aim for the left edge of the fairway. Vice versa for a shot that will reliably go from right to left. Your driving area becomes the entire width of the fairway. Aiming down the middle gives you a margin of error of only half the fairway on either side. Distance is good; in-play is better.

Here's another way you can place your drive in the fairway. When you come to a short par 4 where your 3 wood or 5 wood off the tee will leave you short of trouble and still only a short iron to the green, by all means make this selection. Similarly, on a par 5 where you cannot possibly reach the green in two shots, tee off with a 3 wood. Play your second with a 5 wood or even an iron and have a comfortable short iron to the green. If it's a three-shot hole, why not make it three easy shots?

Getting your tee shot in play certainly produces better scores. Also, it makes your game much more enjoyable by removing anger and frustration—inevitable results of mishit tee shots.

VIDEO

If your golf professional teacher has an instructional video camera, by all means use it. If you have a video camera and a VCR, ask your pro to take pictures of your shot making. This way, you can get the maximum benefit from his instructions. There is nothing that can monitor your progress better than videos of your shot making.

This is the final word. Your instructor is the single most important factor in taking you from a person who plays golf to one who plays golf well.

LEARNING AIDS

There are three reliable sources from which one can learn the *Absolutes* of the basic golf shot:

· A class "A" PGA or LPGA teacher
  This instructional golf book
  A video by a PGA member, explaining the basic golf
     shots

Once you have learned these *Absolutes* and selected any
Variables that suit you, no more information is needed. A
physical routine, practice, and experience are all that is
required to implement your *Variables* and *Absolutes.*

The most positive tool to show that these *Absolutes* are
correctly performed is the video camera. See what you are
doing wrong. Make any necessary corrections at the practice
range. Take another video. Review it for accuracy of performance.

If a picture is worth one thousand words, a video is
worth ten thousand.

Why do millions of golfers spend tens of millions of
dollars each year on their golf games? They buy magazines
that are redundant and contradictory. They buy books with
titillating but unfulfilled promises. Phrases such as "twenty-
minute miracle," "one move to . . . ," "the true secret,"
"golf's miraculous new . . ." are typical. They purchase new
high-tech golf clubs for greater distance. They buy more
expensive golf balls that purport to go farther but don't.

In spite of all this, the golfer does not play better or
score better. Each year the avalanche of data and new equipment grows. Sales rise, but the unfortunate golfer does not
improve.

Why is this so?

This is so because he has not learned what you learned
in the Introduction: "Golf is an unnatural game." He does
not know you do not swing the club; rather, the club is swung

by the turning body. No one has ever told him, or explained, what the *Golf Movement* is. He doesn't know there will be no shot consistency without a routine that is always used.

He has heard "Golf is more than 90 percent mental." No one has told him why or how to deal with this, but you will learn why and how in Part II.

SUMMARY

You should view with skepticism the conflicting information from magazines, books, television, and especially from well-meaning friends.

If you elect to take lessons from a teaching golf professional, it should not be limited to two or three sessions. This should be ongoing as long as you play golf. Many public golf courses and public driving ranges have teaching pros on their staff. Your instructor will become a person who has developed your game and followed its progress. Like going to your family doctor who has all your medical records, your professional will be able to detect errors. He will give you the prescription for getting well.

Find such a person and develop such a relationship.

It is critically important that you see a video of your shot making. A golfer is rarely doing what he believes he is doing. A personal video will instantly show any difference between the perceived and the actual performance.

11.

THE MENTAL GAME

INTRODUCTION

Every golfer needs to know how the mind affects the game. And, more important, how to control and direct its activity.

When practicing, you probably make good shots. When you play the course, you hit good and bad shots with the same club. You play nine holes well and the other nine badly. You play great one day and poorly the next, even though nothing has changed physically.

What causes this dramatic change? The mind, thoughts, and feelings—the final determinants in all shot making. Only when the mind focuses on its predetermined thought—during the entire performance of the physical *Golf Movement*—are good shots made. That is when the body and mind function together, in harmony.

Imagine a work of classical music with a central melody. Secondary melodies weave throughout the performance, creatively positioned in counterpoint to the primary melody. Any one of the secondary melodies, standing alone, has little value. Only in correct combination with the major theme does a work of art result.

The *Golf Movement* is the primary melody. Thoughts and feelings are counterpoint melodies. Correctly combined, they consistently produce a great performance.

Chapter 9

THE BRAIN

Part II begins with the brain and how it functions during your golf shots. Why describe this? Isn't this going to add confusion to a game that already has more than its share?

When you have trouble with your car, you take it to an auto mechanic. When your home electrical system malfunctions, you call an electrician.

Learning how to "fix" your mind when it doesn't perform during your golf shots is imperative. As the man said, "You can't fix it if you don't know why it's broke."

The brain has two sides, two hemispheres, and each deals with different thought processes.

LEFT SIDE (DOMINANT)

Details
Problem Solving
Logic
The Past, the Future

Let's look at just how this works when making a golf shot.

As you arrive at the ball, the left side of your brain is in control. It looks at the ball and then at the target. It considers factors that will affect the shot such as wind and a bad lie. Next, it decides which club will be used and which shot will be made: regular, fade, draw, punch, and so on.

The left side decides where the ball will have to land to place it in the most advantageous position. Finally, it makes any adjustment for avoiding hazards: out of bounds, water, woods. This is the planning stage, which, depending on circumstances, may be simple or complex. The left side of the brain makes these analyses. It is decisive and unequivocal. Then its job is finished.

RIGHT SIDE (SUBORDINATE)

Mental Images
Intuition
The Present

From this point forward, the goal is for the right side of the brain to direct the action. Easier said than done. The dominant left side does not want to give up control. It tries to keep filling your mind with such details as how to perform the shot and what the results will be. Thus, it is not surprising that the critical first step of the mental golf game is training the *right side* to come forward and take control once the *left-side* planning is complete.

This begins with the preshot routine. All planning for the shot has been completed. You stand a few feet behind the ball on the target line. Your grip on the club is fixed but gentle. As you lightly swing the club back and forth, you look at the target. You picture the ball flight to the target. Then you approach the ball, set the club face, and take your stance. Again, look from the ball to the target and back. Perform your *Address Absolutes* and you are ready to begin the *Turnback.*

Easy. But what was in your mind during this procedure? The answer should be *any thought or feeling that is positive:*

"I feel calm . . . unrushed."
"This is my shot . . . I'm really good at this!"

If negative thoughts or feelings interfere, STOP! Start again and establish a positive mental state and retain it throughout your preshot routine.

Now you are ready to begin the *Golf Movement.*

SUMMARY

The brain has a dominant left hemisphere and a subordinate right hemisphere.

The left side deals with details, problem solving, logic, the past, the future, and, therefore, results. Its role is to consider all relevant factors, then decide what shot to make.

The right side of the brain deals with images, intuition, and the present. The right side directs after the left side completes the plan.

Learning to have the right side in complete control during actual shot making is the essence of the mental golf game.

Chapter 10

THE LEARNING
STAGE–STAGE I

There are three progressive stages to your mental golf game.

Stage I is the Learning Stage. Here, your thoughts focus on your physical performance of the *Turnback, Transition,* and *Turnthrough.* You think of the *Absolutes* you learned, the *Variables* you selected. Stage I also applies when learning new and altered shots, e.g., hitting a ball buried in the sand, making pitch shots on greenside heavy rough, and playing from divots.

When learning golf, as in learning anything, you will make mistakes. While you are performing one action correctly, something else will go wrong. This is normal. Your goal is to learn and perform all the *Absolutes*—a goal you can, and will, achieve.

Learning the *Absolutes* of the preshot routine and the *Golf Movement* requires using the left side of your brain. Left-side learning is required before advancing to Stage II, where the right side takes full control.

During Stage I, a video camera and VCR are of tremendous value. As your learning progresses, regular videotaping will let you see what you are actually doing. Compare these tapes against your checklist of *Absolutes* to monitor your progress.

SUMMARY

When learning to play the game or learning new shots, you are in Stage I. During this time, you must concentrate on the physical moves required to learn the particular shot at hand. Consistency is too much to expect at this stage.

Learning all the physical *Absolutes* and accomplishing them as a reflex action (without thought) are prerequisites to Stage II.

Chapter 11

A SINGLE
THOUGHT—STAGE II

Moving from Stage I to Stage II is like giving up your security blanket. In Stage I, thinking about physical action is definitive and complete. You know what you did or did not do, and that's all there is to it. Stage I concentrates on visible and totally understandable tangibles.

What occupies your mind when thoughts of how to perform the *Golf Movement* are no longer needed? This is Stage II. When the right side of the brain takes over from the left, the mind concentrates on a single thought. This can take the form of a mental video, imagery, or a verbal key or phrase. During Stage II, the mind focuses on this thought, in the present, for the duration of the *Golf Movement.*

In Stage I there were no options in learning the physical *Absolutes.* The left side of the brain was in control. Stage II has many options. Your personality, temperament, and genetic qualities combine to help you select the single thought that will work for you.

People are different. What works for one may not work for another. Experiment, but be patient and persevere because finding the single thought that works for you is a prerequisite for success in Stage II.

IMAGERY

From USA Today, *July 16, 1990*

"No bar holds too difficult for 'daring' gymnast [Bill] Roth. To motivate himself, Roth visualizes.

" 'The only way I can become confident about a routine is to see it in my mind first,' he says. 'Before I did my [Festival] vault routine, I had this smile on my face [while] standing there at the end of the runway. For some reason, I just knew it was going to be easy. I've never had that happen before.' "

N O T E

Bill Roth earned four gold medals and an all-around silver at the Olympic Festival.

For some people, imagery will be easy. For others, it will be impossible. The only way to know if imagery will work for you is to experiment.

Ask someone to help you make a videotape of your complete *Golf Movement*—the *Turnback, Transition,* and *Turnthough*—correctly done. Study it at home until you can visualize and remember the total action picture.

Go to the practice range and, as you hit shots, imagine yourself as an outside observer of your own performance. If you can visualize yourself making the complete *Golf Movement,* you have the fortunate ability to create mental images. The video you watched at home has become a mental video.

All that is in your mind during the total time for each shot is your mental video.

If creating a mental video of your complete *Golf Movement* is difficult, you might try a less extensive mental video that could produce equally satisfying results. Again, as an outside observer, visualize a specific portion of the *Golf Movement*, e.g., the *Turnthrough*, in which your lower body starts the action. If you can develop one correct, easily repeatable mental image, use it as your singular thought in Stage II. Don't struggle with this. The ability to create mental images is an aptitude—a genetic gift. If you are not so gifted, select another single-thought process that does not require an associated mental image.

BALL FLIGHT

If mental imagery is not for you, there are other means of creating a positive mental state for the few seconds it is required. Consider the ball-flight thought you had during your preshot routine.

When you look from the target back to your ball, just prior to beginning the *Turnback*, simply focus on the ball going to the target. Exhale, retain this thought, and begin.

This procedure has an added advantage: You do not think of any physical action. Your thought is not of what you are doing (as was necessary in Stage I).

VERBAL KEY

Another mental process some have used successfully is to select a word or two that describes the *Golf Movement*, e.g., fluid, silky, lazy, flowing. Or, in a different vein, turn-turn. This technique is also highly individual. It may take some time and experimentation to identify that single word or two that consistently produces the results you want. Create a singular thought or image—your mantra—that fills your mind for the duration of your *Golf Movement.* This is the foundation of the entire mental game in Stage II.

HOW TO DEVELOP THE MENTAL GAME OF GOLF

Trial and error are time-consuming. Unfortunately, there are no shortcuts to developing the selective thought that will consistently work for you.

Begin on the practice tee. When you are successful there, take your selective-thought process to the course. Play some holes alone or with a friend. If your success continues, arrange a game and try your selective-thought process under normal playing conditions, but *don't expect too much, too soon.*

Learning to play the mental game of golf successfully is much more difficult than learning to play the physical game. Amateurs who shoot 85 or 90 are able to par every hole on the golf course. Their physical game is capable of this. But the lack of single-thought focus during any one round interferes with this accomplishment. Professionals will tell you that more than 90 percent of the game is mental for them. This also holds true for you.

HOW DO YOU KNOW THE MENTAL GAME IS WORKING FOR YOU?

You will know when it is working because your shot is good and you experience a sensation of the ball meeting the club on the sweet spot. Not thin, or heavy, or off center, but "pure." Most of all, you will know because you will be aware that you maintain your thought without interference for 100 percent of the *Golf Movement.*

A Chinese proverb says, "The most important part of a journey is the first step." This is your first step. Initially, if using your selected thought is successful three or four times in a full round of golf, you have done very well. Don't be surprised if these shots occur unexpectedly. You are "out of the hole" and you go to the ball, use your selected thought, and let it happen. Your single thought produced a great shot. "I've got it!" you tell yourself. Don't be disappointed if on your next shot, you don't "got it." With practice and patience, it will return.

WHY DID IT WORK?

Why did this happen? What caused this metamorphic change from your usual shots? The right side of the brain was in control. The left side was shut out. Only positive feelings or sensations were present. Nothing interceded, positive or negative, with your single-thought process.

When developing your single thought, you should remember:

The Mind Is Nondiscriminatory

Between the single-digit and 20 handicapper, the difference in physical skills does not demand an equal difference in mental skills. You may never be able to hit the ball far enough or straight enough to be a scratch player, but nothing is stopping you from developing a scratch mental game.

MAINTAIN YOUR THOUGHT

It is not difficult to begin with the correct thought and maintain it through the *Turnback.* This "getting-set" move only lasts for a second or so. At the apex, where there is a change of direction (or during the *Turnthrough*), the "hit instinct" may surface, causing you to "lose it." You may only lose your thought for a split second, but it's enough to affect the outcome of the shot.

Often, anxiety or concern for the shot's outcome will interfere. A myriad of factors could produce interference—a sound, the wind, an emotion. And remember, the dominant left side of the brain always tries to "run the show" and must be kept out.

Unless you realize it is necessary to sustain your single thought throughout the *Golf Movement,* you are likely to lose focus and not realize this is what causes your missed shots.

As we said before, the single-thought process is developed with practice. Go to your practice area with your single thought as a goal for every shot. Don't concern yourself with where the shots go but with whether you are able to keep your thought for the entire physical action. After each shot, ask yourself, "Did I . . . *focus to the finish?* "

No matter how excellent the shot, your single thought is useless if you have not maintained it 100 percent of the time the *Golf Movement* is occurring.

Finally, the following story should bring home the concept that the mind has the final word in each of your golf shots.

Many years ago, at Pine Valley Golf Club in New Jersey, Owen McManus, a big, strong, happy-go-lucky Irishman, was playing in a foursome that had reached the ninth tee. Owen played golf the way he had played linebacker for Pitt—go up to the ball and whack it! His misadventures on the golf course were legendary. More than a few times his drive struck the tee marker. Once it flew over the back of the tee, down a hill, and onto the Pennsylvania Turnpike. Can you imagine a full swing with a driver sending the ball forcibly between his legs? Owen accomplished this more than once.

Back to the foursome on the ninth tee—Owen was first and sent his drive deep into the woods on the right at a most severe angle from the tee.

A scratch golfer who was only one over par at the time was in the foursome. Owen's outlandish shot caused him to say, "Owen, how could you hit such a terrible shot? It went straight off two hundred yards with an angle of more than forty degrees. A driver can't hit a ball like that!"

The forecaddie was good and, after a brief search, announced he had Owen's ball in the woods.

The scratch golfer was next to tee off. He proceeded to hit his shot. The ball landed four feet from the caddie who was standing in the woods beside Owen's ball.

As they walked off the tee, the excellent player said, "I can't believe it. All I could think of was Owen's shot . . . I actually visualized it in the air when I was making my own."

His score on the hole was a snowman (8), and that was the end of the day for him.

Owen played on, unfazed.

Use this story as a reminder of the irrefutable maxim

You Do What You Think

SUMMARY

Stage II of the mental game is the single-thought stage. Unquestionably, all golfers can reach this stage and consistently give their maximum performance.

The single thought can be developed as imagery, as a mental video, ball-flight visualization, or a special word or phrase. Each is individualistic and learned through trial and error.

Once you have found "your thought" (changeable from time to time), only one edict is required for a strong mental golf game:

Maintain Your Single Thought Until Completion of the Entire *Golf Movement*

A scratch mental golf game is an achievable goal for all golfers.

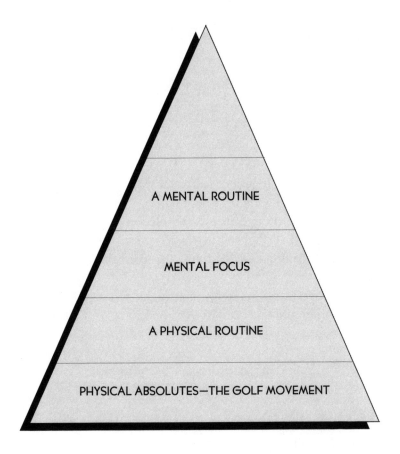

PROGRESSION CHART
GOLF SHOTS

A MENTAL ROUTINE

MENTAL FOCUS

A PHYSICAL ROUTINE

PHYSICAL ABSOLUTES—THE GOLF MOVEMENT

Chapter 12

PERCEPTIONS, FEELINGS, ATTITUDES

Along with developing your single-thought process, you must deal with other influences. Perceptions, feelings or sensations, and emotions can intrude as friend or foe. They can aid, influence, or even destroy your mental process.

PERCEPTIONS

In 1948, Ben Hogan wrote *Power Golf.* Many believe this is the best book ever written about how to play the physical game of golf. It is still available in paperback.

> On page 39 of *Power Golf:*
> "Just before the hands and arms come into play, the body should be set for the hit. By that, I mean that 90% of the weight should be on the left foot."
> And on page 51:
> "My body is set for the hit and 85% of the weight is now on the left foot."

Today, most every golfer on the PGA Tour has more than 50 percent of his weight on the *right* side at impact. Further, those who have the most weight on the right side, such as Greg Norman and Mark Calcavecchia, hit the ball the farthest.

How can this discrepancy (not quantitative but as different as black and white) be reconciled?

Perception.

In the 1940s, no one thought to have golfers stand with each foot on a different scale and measure the weight on each side as they hit golf shots. Today they do.

Ben Hogan had a strong perception that his weight was on the left because of the force of his legs and hips turning left. Without evidence to the contrary, this perception became an intellectual fact.

What is a perception? How is it created? Can it be developed, and, most important, can you develop and use a *positive perception* in your golf game?

A perception is a *single, unified, sensory awareness*.

Single: It is one. You don't want multiples in your mind when making a golf shot.

Unified: a single entity that is a continuum and is whole.

Sensory: a feeling or sensation that is pervasive during the entire **Golf Movement**.

Awareness: Throughout your golf shot or stroke, you're aware of the perception being present.

A perception is a more or less vague sensation. For example, you have a perception that the entire **Golf Movement** is graceful or fluid. Your perception may simply be that your turning body is swinging your **Unit**.

An example of a deeper perception is the following: As you approach the ball from behind the flight path, you have the sense that a nonspecific force will send the ball to the target. You might perceive your spine as a vertical around which the body is going to make a turning-turning action that will cause the ball to go to the target.

FEELINGS/SENSATIONS

Keep in mind that a feeling (or "sensation of") and a thought are two separate mental entities and can coexist during your shot making. Your goal is to have a single thought that generates a positive feeling.

Feelings or sensations appear both in negative and positive forms.

NEGATIVE	POSITIVE
Agitated	Calm
Afraid	Unafraid
Tense	Relaxed
Anxious	Confident
Stressed	Stress-free
Rushed	Unhurried

These sensations are a constant part of your daily life and thoughts. They are able to override, dominate, and affect your thinking and thus your actions.

When positive feelings occur, they are welcome. When negative feelings move in—face, trace, and replace them.

1. **Face:**   Acknowledge their existence.
2. **Trace:**   Identify their source and cause.
3. **Replace:** Find their opposite positive and use it.

Pushing a negative feeling aside or to the back of your mind is not enough. Negative feelings are persistent and, unless replaced with positive feelings, will return.

Face: "Boy, I've really been rushing these last few shots (with predictable results)."

Trace: "It's my good practice sessions. They make me think every shot on the course will be a great one and I can't wait to hit it."

Replace: "I can slow down. There's a foursome in front of us and we're not going to pass them, so why hurry? I'll just walk slower to the ball, take a few deep breaths, and relax my shoulders and arms. Then I'll make my shot without rushing."

Face: "I'm afraid of this 7 iron to the green, even if it is the right club for hitting the ball near the pin. Look at that deep trap just in front of the pin placement."

Trace: "The pin is too close to the trap for me."

Replace:
a. "Why not use a 6 iron? It's a large green, and even if it's not a perfect shot, I'll surely clear the trap."
or
b. "There's an open fairway to the right front and side of this small green. I'll ignore the pin and hit a safe shot to where I can pitch and make a putt for par. Worst case, I'll make an easy bogey."

Remember, negative feelings cannot be pushed aside. Persistent and tough, they will return and destroy your shot. Replace them with positive solutions.

EMOTIONS

An emotion is an intensified feeling.

On TV and in person, members of the PGA Tour are often criticized for showing no emotion. Exceptions like Lee Trevino and Chi Chi Rodriguez are viewed as a refreshing change.

Tour players are "at their office" on the course. This is where they work. This is how they make their living. They have learned that expressing intense feelings for more than a few seconds may affect their mental and physical performance for the rest of the round. Instead, their expression of emotion, good or bad, is minimal—perhaps a hand gesture or facial expression—gone as quickly as it was displayed.

You are not on the Tour. You play golf for fun. Expressing your feelings in a brief and tactful manner is okay. But you should learn from the pros and make this ironclad rule: *Never, never retain an emotion to the point of preparation for the next shot.* If it's still with you, take a few deep breaths, tie your shoes, walk around a bit. Replace it so you can bring your routines into play and focus on your next shot.

ATTITUDES

The feelings and sensations we have discussed are short-lived. They seem to come and go whenever they wish.

Attitudes, however, last. In normal living they may be with you continuously for a month, a year, or longer. During a round of golf, an attitude may be ever-present.

Even if you're playing well, you'll have a miserable time

if you've brought a bad attitude to your round of golf. A good attitude, regardless of your score, will carry you through a pleasant four or five hours.

EXAMPLE: NEGATIVE ATTITUDE

There are people who consistently arrive at the first tee with the same negative attitude that they carry through their day-to-day living. Others, with an otherwise pleasant attitude, undergo a metamorphosis when they play golf.

Is there something about the game of golf that can cause a change in attitude? Yes. The fact is that the average amateur golfer cannot reproduce the good shots of practice for a full eighteen holes. Not understanding (or unwilling to accept) this results in frustration and anger.

Golf is unique. You learned that the length of time between shots, lack of physical movement, and difficulty of long-term focus affect the game of golf from one moment to the next. Acceptance and understanding of these facts can convert a losing attitude into a winning one.

EXAMPLE: POSITIVE ATTITUDE

Golfers with an upbeat approach maintain their positive attitude throughout the round. They encourage their playing companions, accentuate the positive, and eliminate the negative. Their positive attitude directly contributes to a winning team.

There are many stories illustrating the importance of attitude. You certainly have some of your own.

Here is a true story, demonstrating the effects of attitude on the people around you.

Decades ago, before golf was televised, there were not many PGA tournaments and the purses were small. A well-known course in Virginia held an annual event in which a professional played with three amateurs. Because large amounts of money were wagered, the winning professionals appreciated a healthy "payday."

The professional of one particular team was identified as "one of the world's best golfers." His amateur partners were in awe of his credentials and track record when the round began. As play continued, their awe changed to displeasure and then to anger. The pro berated their poor play and failure to use their handicap strokes nonstop.

When the team reached the sixteenth tee, a par 5, their best ball was tied for the lead. A stream ran down the right, and there was a pond in front of the green. Woods lined either side of the fairway and were behind the green.

Two amateurs were quickly out of play. Amateur number three hit two shots and was just short of the pond. The professional hit his typical drive, long and straight down the fairway. He turned to amateur number three and said, "Hit your third shot and see if you can clear the pond." He did. The ball rolled to within three feet of the hole. The green was flat. He had a handicap stroke, so one putt would be an eagle, two putts a birdie.

The pro, now secure, tried for the green on his second shot. The ball went into a marsh over the green. He played a provisional ball into the stream, and neither ball was ever found.

The lone amateur conferred with the other two while the pro was shooting. Then amateur number three walked onto the green and deliberately took five putts. Without a word, the three amateurs walked to the next tee. The pro was dumbfounded. The team finished out of the money.

Thoughts and feelings can be contained. Attitudes cannot. Attitudes rise to the surface through actions or words. As you play, ask yourself if your attitude is a contribution to, or a distraction from, the game.

Summary

There are mental factors other than a single thought. Perceptions, feelings, emotions, and attitudes can coexist or replace your selected thought. All of these may occur as positives or as their opposites—negatives. Negatives only go away when they are replaced with positives.

Attitudes are infectious. Use yours to make your playing companions' game, as well as your own, more enjoyable.

Chapter 13

CONFIDENCE

Confidence is an all-pervasive state that must begin the moment you select the shot. It must continue through the preaddress rehearsal and as you take the address position. This ambience of confidence remains in the background while your single-thought process and *Turnback* take over.

Confidence relates to your mental game the same way relaxation relates to your physical game. Without it, there is no success. (An interesting thought . . . it is confidence that allows one to relax.)

> **From "Quoting 'Em" in the sports section of the *Pittsburgh Post-Gazette:***
> "Jack Nicklaus—when his son Jack II asked him how he developed his confidence: 'You just have it and you go out and do it. There's no developing it.' "

Jack began playing golf some thirty-five or forty years ago and became the best amateur golfer in the world. He won the USGA Amateur Championship in 1959 and 1961.

After that he became a professional and continued to be the best. His victories, particularly in the major championships, testify to that.

For more than a quarter of a century, he has had more success than anyone playing the game. From the beginning, he had success and consequently confidence, which he has retained throughout his career. Is it any wonder he could comment on confidence with "You just have it."

If he's right, what happens to the rest of the golfers who lack confidence? The quality of confidence can be gained by anyone, but the quantity is determined by multiple factors:

> **Skill Level**
> **Amount of Practice**
> **Level of Instruction**
> **Personality**
> **Age**
> **Basic Degree of Confidence**

Confidence is gained with success. "So," you say, "I need success to gain confidence. How do I achieve success?"

Begin small.

SUCCESS– CONFIDENCE

Achieve confidence by doing something doable, something within your range of repeated success. Practice putts from 1 to 1½ feet. Practice chip shots from a good lie to a flat green. Hit wedge shots to a practice green.

The *Success-Confidence* relationship is like a set of ascending stairs. The first step is a small success with a cor-

responding small amount of confidence gained. Each upward step has more success and greater confidence. The successes are accumulative, as is the increase in confidence.

You may say, "That's all well and good for a long-term plan, but what about today? Right now." Set a cardinal rule for yourself: "I will not try a shot in which I do not have confidence *now*."

When a situation calls for a particular shot that gives you the F-A-T-S (Fear, Anxiety, Tension, Stress), don't play that shot! Play another. Every day, thousands of golf shots are missed because the golfer played what he felt was called for instead of a shot he could hit with confidence and success.

One story, repeated thousands of times a day, may have a familiar ring.
Jack Orth, with an 18 handicap, is a golfer at White Cliffs Country Club by the ocean in Plymouth, Massachusetts. Jack, who has been playing golf for only three years, attacks

life (and golf) with a fanatic zeal that has brought him recognition as a decorated war hero, champion tennis player, and world-class salesman.

The White Cliffs course is not difficult, but one par 3 on the back nine is a real challenge. It requires a 190-yard carry over a water-filled marsh. Six-inch-high marsh grass surrounds the green, which has a severe slope back to the marsh. Putting is difficult.

Jack's score was fair to good each time until he came to this hole. Inevitably, he took out a driver and hit the ball in the water. He then played a dropped ball short of the pond. "That ruined my score," he said. "I know I can get over that water." And each time, he'd skull the ball over the green into the marsh grass or hit another into the pond.

His score averaged 6 or 7 on this hole. After the hole was over, he went to the next tee and with relative serenity played the rest of the holes quite well. It was as though he had accepted "paying his dues" to the troll of the marsh.

Jack was not alone. Others in the foursome (as well as those ahead and behind) gave similar performances. By the time Jack and his playing partners reached this tee for the third time, one of the players said to Jack, "Over to the right is a large fairway. You could reach that easily with a 5 or 7 iron. By hitting your tee shot there you'll have only a 9 iron or wedge to the green. You'll be on in two with two putts for a four. A good approach shot or putt and you make a three."

Jack looked startled. "I can reach that green. I've done it before."

In every round of golf you play, you'll have situations that require an "almost-perfect" shot. Don't try that shot. Maintain your composure, continue in a state of calm, and, if you select and execute a shot in which you have confidence, you will certainly have a lower score.

SET AN ATTAINABLE GOAL

Carry the thought of setting an attainable goal for each shot throughout the round. Scorecards are unfair. If you look at your scorecard before a round and the par is 72, that's the right scorecard for someone with a scratch handicap; but how about the golfers with 10 and 20 handicaps?

Do you think you would play better if you had a "personalized" scorecard? If you had a 10 handicap, for instance, the scorecard would show par as one stroke higher for the ten hardest holes. If you were playing *your scorecard for your par* for the entire eighteen holes, the results would surprise you.

Imagine using your own scorecard on a long par 3 with traps all along either side and in the back. *Your* par here is 4. Now you don't need to force a driver or 3 wood (even though an excellent shot would put you on the green). Instead, you play a confident shot some 20 or 30 yards short of the green. With a confident pitch or chip shot, you can par easily and have a good chance of making your birdie.

The value of this mind-set is even more apparent on those tough par 4's—surely a handicap stroke hole for you. But that never occurs to you. You are trying to make par. Your drive is in the rough or a fairway bunker. You want so much to make a par here. Your mind says you need to make that "supershot" of a number 3 iron out of the sand or number 4 wood out of the rough. Undaunted and intent on making a par, you hit a dubbed shot, a wild shot, or, even worse, leave the ball in the sand or the rough!

Compare that to this scenario. It's the same hole, same tee shot, only *your* scorecard has this as a par 5 hole. Now you don't need to try a one-in-a-hundred shot out of the hazard or the rough to get on the green. Instead, take the club that will get you out of trouble and onto the fairway. From there, you comfortably reach the green with a short iron. You're on the green in three—that is regulation. If you make the first putt, you have a birdie. With two putts, you have a par. You walk off the green happy, calm, and relaxed. Your attitude for making your tee shot on the next hole is excellent.

Employ this mind-set and course of action on those long par 5's where *your handicap* makes them par 6.

Try this for two or three rounds. Use a heavy marker to blot out the scorecard pars and put in your own, based on your full handicap. As you reach each hole, check *your par* and play prudently to get on the green in regulation, take two putts (or one), and move on to the next hole. Do this for 18 holes and you will play better, score better, and have a relaxed, pleasant round of golf. You have set attainable goals and only played shots you were truly confident of making.

> P.S. The professionals have par 5 holes they can reach in two shots and then putt for an eagle. Likewise, there will be holes where, with your handicap-marked card, you can putt for eagles. On handicap holes where you can *comfortably* reach the green in less than regulation, by all means do. The key is to be *prudent* and *selective*.

Then there is false confidence.

False confidence is the wee voice that says, "Okay, you can make this shot. Remember? You did it on the practice tee once, so it's possible. Just try real hard." Alarms should go off the moment the wee voice says "once" and "try real hard." Tell the wee voice you're going to play a shot you trust. And do it. If you don't, this is what happens:

Trying "real hard" to make the optimum shot you made "once" causes uncertainty and anxiety when you don't really know how to make it. Suddenly your positive thoughts and feelings have been replaced with concern. The wrong messages are coming to the body from the brain; the muscles tighten; the results are sadly predictable.

Since you're not a robot, you will have bad shots. What happens then?

Gene Sarazen said he expected to miss four or five shots each round—maybe early, maybe late. He didn't worry about it, so he maintained his confidence level throughout the round. Of course, you'll miss some shots. Everyone does. It's part of the game. They happen, and then they're gone. So forget them.

If you have a bad eighteen holes, a bad round, don't rush to the practice tee to change your physical game. Unless the bad round was caused by one obvious, recurring physical error, look instead to your mental game.

Did you bring mental stress to the golf course? Were there distractions that caused you to lose focus on your mental routine? Review the round in your mind. If you're honest with yourself, the cause was probably mental interference. This can be remedied so you can play the next round with confidence.

Keep in mind that confidence can, and does, exist at all levels of play.

Here's a true story of real confidence netting positive results.

Since 1951, twenty-four men have gone to The Cascades Golf Course in Hot Springs, Virginia, each spring for a handicap event.

Jim, a left-hander with an 18 handicap, received a stroke on each hole.

To successfully negotiate the course, Jim needed to slice most of his shots because The Cascades runs counter-clockwise around a mountain. Every time he hit a right-to-left shot, his ball hit the hillside and bounced down to the flat fairway.

For four days, Jim sliced his shots and, with his handicap, beat all the other players.

Confidence? Absolutely. He knew the basic flight the ball would take on every shot. Whether the ball was hit well or not so well, it always went in the direction he planned. The slice took distance off the shots so Jim was consistently short of trouble off the tee and on his shot to the green. Jim is a good putter as well, so you can understand why he was victorious.

This clear example of confidence illustrates that success is assured (1) by playing shots you know you can play, and (2) by playing with no regard for what the scorecard says or how others are playing.

Confidence Is Knowing, Not Hoping

SUMMARY

Confidence in your mental game is as important as relaxation is to your physical game—without it, you cannot make successful golf shots.

The success-confidence sequence is like a series of steps going upward. Success is the first step because confidence is not possible without it. Begin small: short putts, easy chip shots, short-iron shots. With the correct supervision, begin your ascent up the stairway to complete confidence.

Remember F-A-T-S (Fear, Anxiety, Tension, Stress). If any one of this foursome is present, you cannot play a good shot.

The key is to set attainable goals. Your attainable goals are personal, and you must set them for your current level of play.

Confidence is knowing, not hoping.

Chapter 14

ASSURANCE—STAGE III

The final mental stage is within reach of all golfers, regardless of their skill level.

Stage III uses neither specific thought nor imagery. Stage III is an all-pervasive quality and atmosphere of action without awareness.

Trust is an unquestioned, instinctive belief. Confidence implies trust based on past experience. Assurance is absolute confidence. Certainty. The essence of Stage III guarantees assurance through successful integration of trust and confidence.

With assurance . . .

thoughts of how to perform the shot with success are not needed.

With assurance . . .

Fear, Anxiety, Tension and Stress (F-A-T-S) disappear. You know you can make the shot. You are positive of the outcome before the action begins.

With assurance . . .

all moves are unhurried (not to be confused with

fast or slow tempo). The assured player never rushes or changes his normal shot tempo.

With assurance . . .

a state of calm prevails from address until the shot is completed. The player is quietly focused, not intense.

During the paper-tossing exercise in Chapter 1, your interest was the physical action. Your interest now is in the mental action.

How many times have you casually tossed an empty soda can or wad of paper into a receptacle? During a split second, your eyes saw the target and your brain computed the distance, object weight, force, and speed required. And more often than not, the *casual* toss found its mark. This works because there is (1) no time for negative thoughts, (2) no pressure to succeed, and (3) no anxiety interfering with your confidence.

You *completely trusted your brain* to direct the physical action. And it did.

In Stage III, your brain performs the same way during the golf shot. Look at the flight path so the brain knows your target—relax, and *just do it.*

PGA Tour players have been in Stage III and stayed there. They have been in Stage III and snapped out of it, unable to return. They have gone in and out of Stage III in the same round.

Two of the more interesting examples are David Graham's victory at the U.S. Open at Merion in 1981 and Johnny Miller's victory at the U.S. Open at Oakmont in 1973.
Graham's victory performance was as perfect as

humanly possible. In the final round, he not only placed every drive on the fairway and hit every green in regulation, but he stroked every putt correctly. It was almost a robot-like performance. And he won the Open easily.

Johnny Miller had a pregame plan for his final eighteen holes: Birdie every hole on the course. It had rained, and the course was wet. This enabled him to hit his iron shots to the hole nearly every time. He followed his plan. He birdied the first four holes, parred the next three, and made his only bogey on the eighth. (Exit Stage III: Johnny probably allowed thoughts of how well he was doing, and possible victory, to interfere.) On the ninth hole, a short par 5, he was easily on the green in 2 and made another birdie (back to Stage III). On the tenth hole, he made a very good putt and just missed a birdie. He birdied the eleventh, twelfth, and thirteenth holes. On the fourteenth, he made par and on the fifteenth his final birdie. He parred the last three holes for a 63 to win the tournament.

To understand the mind-set a Stage III player has for all his shots, as compared to the Stage I and Stage II player, consider this example of a chip shot from just off the green.

The Stage I player thinks about how much his wrists must cock, how far back to take the club, and so on. He "hopes" to get the ball on the green to a point from which he can get down in two putts.

The Stage II player focuses on his single thought. Because he has confidence (but not absolute assurance), he expects the ball will stop within two feet of the hole.

The Stage III player checks the green contours and sights the path and distance the ball must travel. He goes to the ball and absolutely expects that when he chips the ball onto the green it will roll into the hole.

Not surprisingly, there are players who consistently hit accurate tee shots, always with assurance. Their iron play is poor (as is their putting), so although they are in Stage III when hitting their drives, once they make this shot they are out of Stage III for the rest of the hole. Similarly, there are players who are only in Stage III when playing iron shots or when putting.

Keep in mind that the Stage III mind-set comes and goes. It is not an all-or-nothing condition.

In Stage II it is difficult to maintain a single thought for every shot made during your round of golf. You are not a machine. When there is interference to your one thought, the result will probably be a missed shot.

In Stage III there is no thought to maintain. Instead, there is a general mental state, without specific thought, which needs to be kept for two seconds or so as each shot is made.

Achieving Stage III is similar to progressing from Stage I to Stage II. You need faith in yourself, practice, and patience.

Have faith . . . Stage III is obtainable. Stage III brings consistency of play at your highest achievable level of performance.

Practice, giving up the single thought that served you well in Stage II. Practice at the driving range, on the practice tee, and in actual play.

Be patient . . . if in the beginning you make only a few shots with Stage III, you are on your way and the rest will follow.

Why not skip Stage II? If you are accomplished in transcendental meditation or more like Uncle Charlie, perhaps you can. For most, however, the natural progression is needed.

Why go into Stage III if you are doing fine in Stage II? Does "doing fine" mean you perform your physical game to your maximum capability every time? Does "doing fine" mean you have total consistency of shots and scores throughout your golf games? Does "doing fine" mean you are absolutely satisfied with your performance?

If you can answer yes to *all* these questions, by all means be content with Stage II.

If you elect to move to Stage III, when will you know you are there?

Your shot will be excellent. Beyond that you will discover a totally new sensation—it will feel right—calm, weightless, effortless. A sense of absolute completeness and perfection will conclude each shot.

A golfer receiving lessons from Bob Ford asked, "Bob, what do you think about when you're making your golf shot?"

Bob thought for a second, then answered, "Nothing."

SUMMARY

Stage III is an all-pervasive mental ambience of action without thought.

Assurance is absolute confidence, certainty. With assurance, no specific thought is needed but rather a state of mind.

There is no fear, anxiety, tension, or stress because the outcome is known before the action begins.

Stage III is accessible to all players who have achieved Stage II.

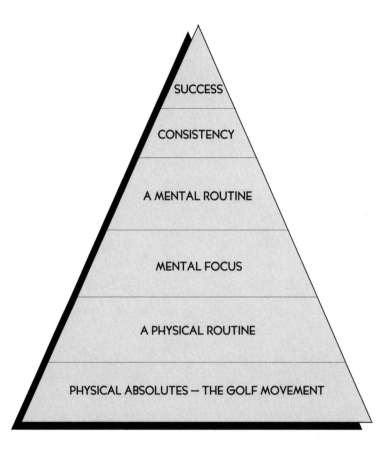

III.

PUTTING

Chapter 15

PREPARATION

INTRODUCTION

Putting is a game within a game. Its performance is independent of the gender, size, strength, or age of the golfer. Poor golfers can learn to be very good putters. All one needs are sound fundamentals, practice, experience, and knowledge of the hows and whys of putting. This will change uncertainty into confidence and confidence into assurance. The means to accomplish this will be detailed in the following chapters.

Many of the characteristics of putting mirror what you have learned about full golf shots.

Putting . . .

has *Absolutes* and *Variables*
has physical and mental parts that must be synchronous
requires strong physical and mental routines
has a set-stroke action
has club-head acceleration through the ball

    is subject to mental interference
    has need for focus throughout the stroke
    requires practice to improve
    ultimately needs only correct direction and distance

PREPARATION

Putting begins when you prepare to make your shot to the green. The location from where you play this shot is immaterial; it could be the fairway, the rough, or a hazard. You are looking for the preferred putting position on the green—the area from which you will most likely sink your first putt. It is also the area from which, should your first putt miss, you will have a tap-in.

For most right-handed putters, an uphill break, or uphill right-to-left break, is most desirable. This, however, is a part of the game that is 100 percent personal.

Let experience teach you where your preferred area is.

A ten-foot putt in which you have confidence has more chance of being holed than a five-foot putt of uncertainty.

Closest is not always best.

A few simple examples might help explain this ball-to-green positioning concept.
Assume in each case that the pin position is in the center of the green. At Oakmont Country Club, the greens are always PGA Tournament fast. The first green slopes away from the players so a shot to the green that goes past the hole makes a much easier first putt, i.e., uphill.

The second hole is just the opposite, with the green sloping severely back toward the fairway. A shot here, past the hole, leaves a putt so treacherous the player is better off to have his ball short of the green with an uphill chip or long putt.

The third hole presents a different problem. The apron and green in the front go decidedly uphill. From there the slope is gently downhill. An uphill-to-downhill chip or putt here is too difficult. The play should be long, with a putt or chip back to the hole.

A PREPUTTING PROCEDURE

As you come onto the green, try to approach your ball from past the hole and look back at the ball. By doing this, you will be able to get a much more accurate reading of the green's slopes and contours.

As you walk to your ball, pause briefly at the hole. See what your ball will be doing the last 8 or 10 inches before it rolls into the hole. Because of its slowing pace, the ball is most susceptible to the green's contours at this distance.

If your putt has a side slope, as you walk from the hole to your ball, always walk on the lower side of the slope and look uphill. This will give you the proper reading of the degree of the slope.

It cannot be overstated that this entire procedure should in no way interfere with other players or be time-consuming. It is simply the way you routinely learn to approach your ball before putting, whenever it is practical.

ROUTINE

Your preshot physical routine begins after (1) you have reached the green, (2) decided on the line, (3) taken your putter in hand, and (4) come to the ball.

It is unimportant *what* your routine is. It is only important that you use it *exactly* for *every putt.*

Putting is, after all, a rather simple action. As such, it should follow that having and using a routine is easy. This is not so. There are disturbing factors in putting that do not exist during the *Golf Movement.* Overall physical movement relaxes. In putting, the lower body and head must be still. The proximity of other players may be disruptive or intimidating. Realizing that the putt finalizes the score may produce anxiety. A putt usually decides who wins or loses the hole.

Whatever routine you finally select, it must contain these three tenets:

1. You are comfortable.
2. It is brief and simple.
3. You can repeat it the same way each time.

What follows is a sample routine. Each action makes a positive contribution.
Shrug your shoulders to make certain they are relaxed. Tight shoulders cause missed putts.
Make a practice stroke. This aids relaxation and confidence.
Breathe deeply with your diaphragm. This is another aid to relaxing.
Squarely align the putter face behind the ball on the target path.
Take your stance.
Exhale. Begin your stroke at a standard interval after exhaling.
This routine creates a solid foundation for the putting *Absolutes* discussed in the next chapter.

Summary

Putting is a game within a game.

Poor golfers can learn to be good putters.

Putting has many of the characteristics of the *Golf Movement.*

Putting begins when you prepare to make your shot to the green.

Learn the type of putt you favor, and try to position your ball for that putt.

It is imperative to have a preshot routine. Its features are not important; its exact use for each putt is important.

Chapter 16

PUTTING ABSOLUTES

Now you are at your ball, preparations and procedures complete, ready to stroke it into the hole. Though there are *Variables* to be addressed, first consider these *Absolutes*.

HOLD STILL!

The phrase "a living statue" is certainly a contradiction in terms, but your body should perform as a living statue during the putt. Your *Unit* (shoulders, arms, hands, putter) makes the putting stroke; your body, from the waist down and from the neck up, remains stationary throughout the stroke. As your *Unit* makes this stroke, your relaxed torso is also free to move and does so.

Your face alignment does not move. If you do not move your face position, nothing above your neck will move. Your lower body (although it will not have a tendency to move) is also immobile.

A putt must be so accurately struck that any unnecessary movement will most likely cause a miss. Unfortunately, when putting, many golfers move without realizing it. Have someone make a video of your putts during a round of golf—you will be amazed at the number of times you missed a putt solely because you moved. A more practical, although less satisfactory, procedure would be to have your caddie or one of your playing companions check to see if you move during the putting stroke. Players miss many more putts because they move than because they selected an incorrect line.

If you continue to move incorrectly, here are two suggestions, either one of which might solve your problem:

First, after striking the putt, look at the slight indentation in the ground beneath where the ball had been resting. This will be clearly visible. Look at this spot after the ball has been struck.

Second, after the ball is struck, mentally count "one, two" before looking up.

GRIP PRESSURE

The second putting *Absolute* is correct and constant grip pressure. This may seem obvious for an *Absolute,* but its very simplicity causes it to be overlooked. Just like incorrect movement, a too tight grip or increased grip pressure during the stroke will cause missed putts. And, as with not holding still, this can occur again and again without player awareness.

What is the correct grip pressure? In a word, the pressure should be light. It should be secure but gentle. Employ the slight amount of hand pressure you would use if you cupped a small bird in your hands or the grip pressure you use on the steering wheel of your car when driving leisurely along the highway. On a scale of 1 to 10, this would be a 3 or a 4.

The old bugbears of fear and anxiety can involuntarily and unknowingly cause your fingers to tighten. When this happens, the club face will turn and the putt will miss. On the practice putting green, this malady is nonexistent. It only appears as a result of on-course pressure.

When you miss putts, ask yourself, "Did my hand pressure increase?"

RHYTHM

The third *Absolute* is rhythm. Rhythm describes a motion that is regular and has a slow and fast action. This is an exact description of the correct putting stroke: regular but slow back and faster forward.

Amateurs and professionals frequently use the word "tempo" to describe the putting stroke. The principal meaning of tempo is speed or rate of motion. Thus, you have "the speed of the stroke." The problem is that there is not one speed, there are two different speeds. The speed back is slower, about half of the forward speed. A putting stroke with rhythm has two speeds—slow and then fast—to create club-head acceleration.

ACCELERATION

The final putting *Absolute* is, not surprisingly, club-head acceleration.

This is a critically important factor in achieving consistently accurate putting.

Relative to the back stroke, there are only three forward strokes: These are decelerating, constant, and accelerating.

Deceleration occurs for two reasons, one physical, one mental. Instinct warns the golfer who has taken the putter back too far. It says, "Ease up, or you'll knock the ball far past the hole." The golfer listens, unconsciously decelerates, and hits a putt with a "dead" roll. The ball floats or drifts off the intended line. The mental cause of decelerating the putter blade is fear. Fear of hitting the ball so far past the hole that the next putt will miss causes the golfer to ease up. This results in a push or shove stroke with the ball ending short and/or to the right of the hole.

A constant tempo stroke would require a pendulum swing of the putter. The speed and distance in each direction would be exactly the same. The metronome-like exactness of such a stroke makes it impractical. On long putts, the distance the putter would have to travel would make consistent accuracy impossible.

You must accelerate the putter head through the ball so it will *roll end over end for its entire journey.*

As the ball approaches the hole, its speed slows. It is imperative at this time that the ball continue its end-over-end track.

A ball rolling in this manner will literally dive into the hole. A ball that has been mis-hit, pushed, or pulled will have side spin as it slows, causing it to turn away from the hole. Even if it hits the hole, it will likely spin out.

A program for learning an accelerating putting stroke will be presented at the beginning of the next chapter.

SUMMARY

There are four putting *Absolutes:*

1. Hold still. From the waist down and from the neck up, move nothing.

2. Your grip on the putter must be light but secure. Never increase this grip pressure during your stroke.

3. Every putt you make must have the same regular rhythm. The back stroke is slower than the forward stroke. The distance of the stroke varies; the rhythm does not.

4. A slower back, faster forward stroke automatically creates club-head acceleration. This acceleration is what causes the ball to roll end over end and thus hold its line into the hole.

Chapter 17

THE PUTTING
STROKE

How could someone learning to putt be anything but confused after watching Chi Chi Rodriguez and Gary Player and then Lee Trevino and Ben Crenshaw? The first two have a quick, short, jab stroke. The other two use a long, slow, fluid stroke. All four players are great putters and have been for many years. Each has a style that is a personal evolution. Thousands of hours on the putting green and on the course have brought them to this point.

You are an amateur. If you play two or three times a week, you are lucky. What you need is a technique that

uses the four *Absolutes*
is easy to learn
is easy to repeat
assures success

The basis of such a technique is to create a stroke whose length and time are correct for the distance the ball must travel.

Obviously, such elements as green speed and putter weight will vary. Use our figures only as beginning reference points.

STROKE DISTANCE

Go to your practice green and step off about 4 feet from the hole. Mark this with a tee or coin. Place a ball beside this marker. Place another tee on the same line about 5 inches farther from the hole.

Take your address. Make the putt, taking your putter back only as far as your 5-inch marker. Repeat this exercise a number of times until you perform it effortlessly.

The distance the putter travels is short. Generating enough force to roll the ball into the hole requires accelerating the putter head through impact. When you don't, the ball is short and usually off line. When you do, there is a dominant sensation. That sensation is club-head acceleration.

When you successfully make putts from the 4-foot range on level and contoured greens, move to longer putts. For an 8-foot putt, place your second marker about 8 inches behind the first. For a 30-foot putt, the distance between the markers is about 15 inches.

STROKE TIME

The time of the back stroke is twice the time of the forward stroke.

The time it takes for the putter head to travel from the

ball to its back-stroke apex is twice as long as it takes the putter head to return to the ball.

As you practice this stroke speed and distance formula, the two parts will blend harmoniously and without effort. For this reason, learning will be easy, as will retention.

THE STROKE

You now have a technique for stroke distance and stroke time. What of the stroke itself? Is it made with the wrists or the shoulders?

In the last half century there has been an evolution in ball striking. It has changed from an arms-wrists-hands swinging of the club to a body-turning *Golf Movement.* Similarly, an evolution has occurred in putting. In the past, a wrist stroke was used for putting. Today almost all members of the LPGA and PGA tours use a shoulders-dominant stroke. Which should *you* use?

Once again, you must make your personal selection through trial and error. Go to the practice green. Maintaining your time and distance stroke parameters, begin by trying each of the two extremes.

Perhaps you will have the touch and feel of Bobby Locke or Billy Casper. Their method was a total wrist action. The cocking wrists brought the putter back. Uncocking the wrists created the through stroke.

A word of caution about this method. Because of the hand sensitivity required, controlled nerves and absolute confidence are necessary on each putt. It is not difficult to be a star on the practice putting green.

At the other end of the spectrum is a stroke made with

almost no wrist action. Here the shoulders and arms form an inverted triangle. The apex (the hands) holds the putter. The triangle simply moves back and then forward with the hands in a locked position. The theory is that there is less chance of error with fewer moving parts. Also, the big muscles of the shoulders are easier to control than the sensitive fingers. This is particularly true for the high-pressure putting required on the professional tours.

THE TAP METHOD

We would like you to consider an alternate method that largely eliminates the principal negative of each of the other two methods: the hands rolling or pronating, the shoulders causing a push or shove stroke.

The dictionary gives us:

"tap, *v.*, 1. to strike or touch lightly. 2. . . . with light blows . . . 6. a light blow or rap."

Here is how to perform this putting method:

1. At address, the majority of your weight is on the left side.
2. Your hands are a little forward.
3. The backward stroke is made with the shoulders and the club head is taken back slightly upward.
4. The forward stroke is made exactly as you would tap a tack with a tack hammer. The beginning of the stroke is unhurried, even slow, because the acceleration occurs only as the putter head contacts the ball.

5. The putter head does not stop on impact; its momentum carries it past the ball.

For this putting method, the distance back is always greater than the distance forward.

SUMMARY

The basis of a correct and repeatable putting method is stroke distance and stroke time.

Once this is established, the player usually putts with a predominantly shoulders or hands stroke.

Our recommendation is to putt with the tap method.

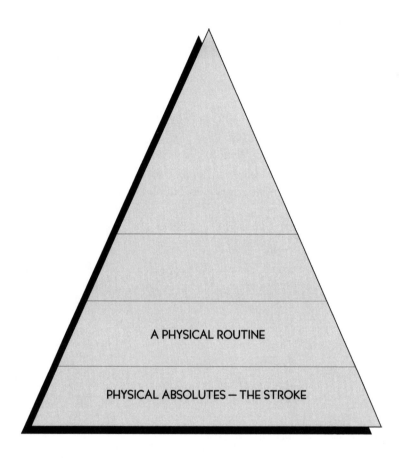

Chapter 18

THE MENTAL
GAME

The Men's, Women's, and Senior PGA tours are much more putting contests than they are ball-striking contests. PGA professionals do not fade from the scene because of their shot making. Physical-fitness awareness and high-technology golf equipment have seen to this. Rather, the inability to be competitive on the green sends them into retirement or, at best, well back in the field.

The reason for this cannot be physical because on Monday these same pros can go to the practice putting green and roll putt after putt into the hole.

Full golf shots are influenced by the golfer's size, age, strength, sex, and genetic qualities. These are relatively meaningless variables in putting. This is because *putting is a mental game.* The thrust of this chapter centers on how to deal successfully with this critical part of your golf game.

Confidence is the ultimate answer and will be discussed at length in the next chapter. There are, however, concrete procedures that will aid you in building a solid mental putting game.

You have created a physical routine for your putting. Now create a mental routine—exactly as you did with your full golf shots.

You are standing behind your ball, ready to make your putt. Your physical routine has begun and is proceeding without thought. You will perform your putting *Absolutes,* and your selected stroke has now become automatic.

What is in your mind?

You look at your ball and visually and mentally trace the path it will take into the hole. Your eyes come back along this line. You take your stance and place the putter head behind the ball. Once again you look at the ball's track and unhurriedly bring your eyes back to the ball. There is an instantaneous pause while you focus on the ball's total path. Picture this total path picture in your mind. Nothing more is needed for correct distance (remember tossing the empty can?). As this one picture fills your mind, you make your stroke. During the back stroke and the forward stroke, this ball path is your only thought.

As the putter impacts the ball, *your mind actually sees the ball rolling on this path into the hole.*

Only when your putter has stopped moving do you look up and walk forward to take your ball out of the hole.

The reasons for the success of this mental putting procedure are, not surprisingly, the same as those for the mental part of the *Golf Movement.*

The right side of the brain is totally in control.
There is a mental image—a mental picture.
There is only one thought.
The thought is positive.
The strong focus excludes all negatives.

Thought is in the now, not in the future or in the results.

All you need now is confidence. This is the subject of the next chapter.

SUMMARY

Putting is ultimately a mental game.

From the time you address your ball until the putter has stopped moving, you have only one thought: *Your mind sees the ball rolling on its selected path into the hole.*

The same mental qualities that made your *Golf Movement* a success make your putting successful: Focus on one thought.

PUTTING

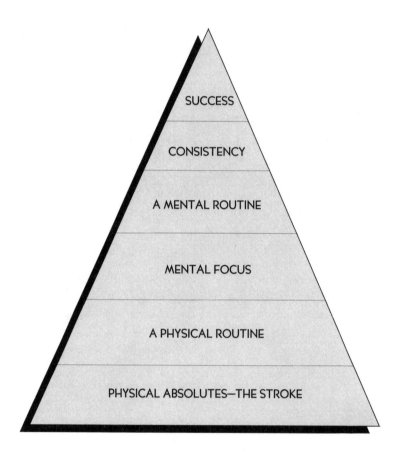

SUCCESS

CONSISTENCY

A MENTAL ROUTINE

MENTAL FOCUS

A PHYSICAL ROUTINE

PHYSICAL ABSOLUTES—THE STROKE

Chapter 19

PUTTING WITH CONFIDENCE

Confidence . . .

> Confidence is *not* something you learn.
> Confidence *is* a by-product of having learned.
> Confidence develops as a pervasive mental state that
> increases as you learn and skill improves.
> Confidence, ultimately, is the product of successful
> performance.

In Chapters 15 through 18 you learned everything you need to be a successful putter. Now you need to create a regimen for using this information on every putt.

Confidence begins when easy, familiar actions are repeated. This means creating a putting-green procedure that is always used for pregame practice or full practice sessions.

Practice Putting Plan
If you are practice putting just prior to playing, use two or three balls. If you are going for a full practice session, use at least six, but not more than ten.

Always use your preputt routine for every putt. Do *not* putt at the hole initially. Simply work on your *Absolutes.* Take your grip, hold still, and practice your rhythm. Putt the balls without concern for direction or distance. Continue this until you produce your rhythm stroke correctly for each putt. Next, practice your thought. Again, do *not* putt at a hole. Just pick a spot on the green and work on mentally seeing the ball roll on its path to this spot. Initially, this rhythm and thought exercise may take ten or fifteen minutes. In time this will lessen substantially.

Now you are ready to practice putting at a hole. During this time, work on your stroke distance and stroke time. Using your preputt routine, begin at the 2-foot range. Putt all the balls from the same spot. You must make all the putts. If you miss, begin again. Start over with ball 1. Once successful, move to another side of the hole and repeat the same procedure. After success here, move to the 3-foot range and then the 4-foot range. Repeat the procedure.

If time permits, practice uphill, downhill, and sidehill putts in the 2-to-4-foot range.

End every practice session with longer putts—five or six from about 15 and 30 feet.

Why is this procedure successful?

What do you think the mind-set and confidence level will be for the golfer who has a long putt and knows, should he miss, that he can certainly make the next putt of less than four feet?

The next step in developing confidence is to move from the practice green to the golf course. This may cause some trepidation; you know the optimum conditions of the practice green will not be equaled on the course.

How, then, are you able to have the practice-green confidence carry over to the actual play? Say to yourself, "I will use my preputt routine. I will use my *Absolutes* and my single thought. I will focus on this *without regard for results.* This is the most that I can do to cause the ball to roll into the hole. Any additional effort, physical or mental, will be counterproductive." Why will this increase confidence? Following this line of thinking will cause you to make a correct stroke each time. Correct strokes make the ball roll into the hole.

You are gaining confidence, but what is going to move you up the success/confidence stairway? Experience will bring you more success. More and more of your putts will drop. You will perform your physical actions automatically each time. You will use your single thought with comfort and confidence. Your ability to accurately read greens will improve the more you play.

At this level of confidence, misses you cause (versus those caused by such elements as terrain and weather) will almost certainly be the result of mental interference. The most common interruption is anxiety about results. When you become aware of this, STOP. Begin again and focus strongly on your ball rolling on its path into the hole.

In the past you approached putts with uncertainty. Now you expect to make putts—and you do. Your confidence is growing, but how can you tell when you have reached the highest plateau of confidence?

As you approach each green, you are positive and excited. Each hole presents a new challenge, a new game. You win the game when you sink the putt. Because you are a good putter, you frequently win. Winning is fun. Even when you miss, your enthusiasm continues and you are eager to get to the next green.

When you walk onto the green, you think, "I'm sure I can roll that ball right into the hole." You are there. You are on the confidence summit. And because everything you are doing is correct, *you will stay there.*

SUMMARY

Confidence is not something you learn. Confidence is a pervasive mental state that develops as a by-product of having learned.

The learning process begins when you create and use a procedure for putting-green practice. Success here builds confidence. Your next step is on-course putting. During this period you focus on performing your preputt routine and your *Absolutes.* You hole more putts. Your confidence increases. Soon you perform your physical actions by rote; you use your single thought with each putt.

You approach each green in a positive state. You expect to make putts—and you do. You have arrived at the putting confidence summit.

IV.

FINAL THOUGHTS

Chapter 20

A WORD ON
WINNING

The paradox of winning is that the more you think about it the less likely it is to happen. This is particularly true of golf, in which time to think and the mental game are so predominant.

What kind of game is golf? What are the characteristics that make it different from other sports? How does one deal with these distinctions?

Competitive sports fall into three basic categories: body contact, mutual object, and personal performance.

Body-contact contests like boxing and wrestling are determined by physical contact. You can win by your actions alone, i.e., by physically overpowering your opponent.

Mutual-object games are characterized by you and your opponent(s) striking or throwing a common object, usually a ball. Here your action alone cannot decide the winning or losing. You may make an excellent shot, your very best, and your opponent may make an even better play and you will lose. In body-contact sports, winning is almost totally under your control. One might say "same object" games are about 50 percent under your influence.

Personal performance contests can range from minimal physical movement (bowling and golf) to continuously strenuous bodily activities (marathon and triathlon). In these sports you can do your lifetime best and not win because you have no control over your opponent's performance. It is very important to understand this fact so all your energies will be directed toward your own performance.

THE GOLF COURSE

In medal-play golf, your opponent is *not* the other player as much as it is the golf course you are playing. To beat this static opponent requires pregame and even prehole planning. This thinking should apply to the very good players as well as those with higher handicaps. Where are the out-of-bounds? Where are the woods or water hazards? Are there some holes where using a number 3 wood or even an iron off the tee would be a prudent play? Are the par 5's reachable in two shots, or must you take three? Are the greens so trapped in the front that a number 5 or number 7 wood would be a more sensible club than a 2 iron? Just as a boxer or tennis player strongly increases his chance of beating his opponent by considering his strengths and weaknesses, so you will increase your chances of beating your opponent— the golf course—by preplay course management and planning.

Match-play golf has declined notably in recent years, but it still exists and has its own characteristics, and it requires a different style of play from the more common medal play.

The cardinal rule in match play is that each hole is

totally separate—like a game unto itself. Scoring a 12 is the same as scoring a 5 if you lose the hole; scoring a 5 is the same as scoring a 3 if you win the hole. The point is, no matter how poorly or how well you play a hole—no matter what the results are—erase this from your mind as you come to the next tee. Each new hole is a new game.

In match play, you may need to be more aggressive or more conservative based on

handicap strokes you or your opponent receive
your opponent's bad or good shots
luck: his or yours—good or bad

The last word on match play is that you must constantly be prepared for the unexpected. Keep a tight rein on your emotions so that before, during, and after the unforeseen occurs you will be composed.

PRESSURE

F ACT

Winning Is a Result of Dealing with Pressure Successfully

When you are playing checkers with your five-year-old daughter or nine holes of golf in the evening with your spouse, you are in a game and people play games to win. But how ambivalent your feelings are! These are people you love, and you want them to have success. Winning for you in this situation is unimportant. This brings us to the first of two principles that illustrate the relationship between pressure and winning.

PRINCIPLE #1

The amount and degree of pressure is exactly proportionate to how important winning is to *you*.

Two players, each with a 20 handicap, come to the last hole, a long, hard par 4, needing to make a 5 to break 90 for the first time. Player number one has been playing for thirty years and never shot in the 80's on a regulation golf course. He loves the game, reads the books and magazines, plays in the rain, wind, cold—and he *really* wants to break 90.

Player number two is young, only began playing last year, and has realistic expectations of playing in the high 70's and low 80's in a few years.

Since *all pressure is self-imposed,* player number 1 is under great pressure while player number 2 has very little, if any, pressure.

Remember, pressure is personal and very real. The player who comes to the last three holes needing three 5's to break 90 for the first time, the golfer who is one up with three holes to play for the club championship, the pro who only needs to "par in" on the last three holes to win his first major championship . . . all feel exactly the same kind of pressure. To be successful, all must deal with their pressure in the same way.

PRINCIPLE #2

When mental pressure develops, the player does one of two things: He plays worse or he plays better. Rarely does he play the same.

There are five rules for joining *the minority* who improve at pressure time:

Rule 1. Don't use left-brain thinking. Have no thought of the future, winning, or results. Use right-brain thinking, in the *now.* Think only of the golf shot you are playing.

Rule 2. Be a Boy Scout—be prepared. Don't let a pressure situation suddenly occur like a thunderclap or you will surely panic. Before you begin your round, realize that these times will come, often unexpectedly. Be prepared to deal with them with equanimity. Don't lose your cool!

Rule 3. Trust and use your routines, physical and mental. It took you a lot of time and work to develop them. You know they produce the results you want—don't desert them.

Rule 4. A hallmark of winners is the more important the shot, i.e., the greater the pressure, the more intensely they focus. They retain their intensity of focus on their singular mental process until they complete the shot.

Rule 5. Slow everything down! There will be an adrenaline rush that will cause your physical movements to be fast, hard, and quick and your thoughts to tumble pell-mell over one another. Counter this by consciously slowing everything. Walk slower; breathe slower and more deeply with your diaphragm. Have a perception that your total *Golf Movement* will have a slower tempo.

The player who has learned and uses the five rules for playing under pressure is capable of giving his peak performance—the most he can do to affect the outcome of the contest.

The penultimate word in learning to win is that it takes practice and experience. Along the way there will be losses, but they provide a necessary service. You rarely learn anything when you win—you always (or should) learn when you lose. Analyze those things you did that contributed to the loss so you will not repeat them.

The final word about winning is the same for success in any endeavor: *will*. Have the determination and the resolve, regardless of the opposition or the difficulties, to make every shot a quality shot. This is truly an intangible, but one of such overwhelming force that its successful use can overcome many negatives and many obstacles. Even though other positive factors are present, winning is highly unlikely without a will to win.

SUMMARY

Winning is a goal that cannot be reached by thinking about it.

In golf you play against two opponents: one stationary—the golf course; one cerebral—mental pressure.

Winning against the golf course requires pregame preparation and planning.

Defeating pressure has two principles and five rules:

Principle 1. The amount of pressure is proportionate to how important winning is to *you*.

Principle 2. When pressure comes, winners play better and losers play worse.

Rule 1. Think only of the shot you are playing.
Rule 2. Be prepared for the unexpected.
Rule 3. Trust and use your routines.
Rule 4. The more important the shot, the greater the focus required.
Rule 5. Slow everything down.

Losses are a necessary part of learning how to win.

Will is the mind's greatest intangible force. It is like the queen in chess—far more powerful than any other piece. A strong sustained will to win is the hallmark of all consistent winners.

Chapter 21

CONCLUSION

THE FINAL FOUR

1. Create a preshot physical routine. Use it religiously on all standard shots.

2. The spine is an axis around which the body revolves. The spine turns, but does not move vertically or laterally.

3. Don't swing the golf club with your arms and hands. The golf club is swung by the body turning clockwise and then counterclockwise.

4. The *Unit* is passive at address, during the *Turnback*, through the entire *Transition*, and to that point midway into the *Turnthrough* when the "good-hit instinct" occurs and activates the *Unit*.

THE MIND GAME

A successful mental game begins once you have developed a correct physical game. Then, as you look at each shot to be played, you think, "I can do this." This confidence produces a positive state of mind. You relax, and an ambience of calm is automatically created.

You select a club, and as you approach the ball and take your address position, you superimpose your preshot mental routine on your preshot physical routine.

You have one thought and/or sensation—your golfing mantra—which performs in concert with your *Turnback-Contra-Turnthrough* technique.

Practice and playing experience will enhance your skills and refine your mental focus.

You now have a correct and complete game that is certain to give you many hours of enjoyment in your golfing future.

Alliss, Peter, and Paul Trevellion. *Easier Golf.* New York: A. S. Barnes, 1970.

Armour, Tommy. *How to Play Your Best Golf All the Time.* New York: Simon and Schuster, 1953.

Blake, Mindy. *The Golf Swing of the Future.* New York: W. W. Norton, 1973.

Boomer, Percy. *On Learning Golf.* New York: Alfred A. Knopf, 1946.

Boros, Julius. *Swing Easy, Hit Hard.* New York: Harper & Row, 1965.

Borysenko, Joan, Ph.D. *Minding the Body, Mending the Mind.* Reading, Mass.: Addison-Wesley, 1987.

Cotton, Henry. *The Game of Golf.* London, Eng.: Country Life Limited, 1948.

———. *Henry Cotton Says.* London, Eng.: Country Life Limited, 1962.

Cousins, Norman. *Anatomy of an Illness.* New York: W. W. Norton, 1979.

———. *The Healing Heart.* New York: W. W. Norton, 1983.

Cranford, Peter G. *The Winning Touch in Golf.* New York: Prentice-Hall, 1961.

Demaret, Sarazen Suggs. *Your Short Game.* New York: Harper & Row, 1959.

———. *Your Long Game.* New York: Harper & Row, 1970.

Editors of *Golf* magazine. *America's Golf Book.* New York: Charles Scribner's Sons, 1970.

Edwards, Betty. *Drawing on the Right Side of the Brain.* Los Angeles, Calif.: Jeremy P. Tarcher, 1989.

Ellis, Wes, Jr. *All Weather Golf.* Princeton, N.J.: D. Van Nostrand Co., 1967.

Ford, Doug. *How I Play Inside Golf.* New York: Prentice-Hall, 1960.

———. *The Wedge Book.* New York: Cornerstone Library, 1963.

Gallwey, Timothy W. *The Inner Game of Golf.* New York: Random House, 1979.

Galvano, Phil. *Secrets of the Perfect Golf Swing.* New York: Prentice-Hall, 1974.

Garfield, Charles A. *Peak Performance.* New York: Jeremy P. Tarcher, 1984.

Haultain, Arnold. *The Mystery of Golf.* New York: Serendipity Press, 1965.

Hebron, Michael. *See and Feel the Inside Move the Outside.* Smithtown, N.Y.: Rost Associates, 1984.

———. *The Art and Zen of Learning Golf.* Smithtown, N.Y.: Rost Associates, 1990.

Herold, Don. *Love That Golf.* New York: A. S. Barnes, 1952.

Hogan, Ben. *Power Golf.* Cranbury, N.J.: A. S. Barnes, 1948.

———. *Five Lessons—The Modern Fundamentals of Golf.* Turnbull, Conn.: Golf Digest and Tennis, Inc., 1957.

Jones, Robert Tyre, Jr. *Golf Is My Game.* New York: Doubleday, 1959.

———. *Bobby Jones on Golf.* Garden City, N.Y.: Doubleday, 1966.

Kelley, Horner. *The Golfing Machine.* Seattle, Wash.: Star System Press, 1969.

Kostis, Peter. *The Inside Path to Better Golf.* New York: Golf Digest and Tennis, Inc., 1982.

Leadbetter, David. *The Golf Swing.* Lexington, Mass.: The Stephen Greene Press, 1990.

Loehr, James E. *Mental Toughness Training for Sports.* Lexington, Mass.: The Stephen Greene Press, 1982.

Lohren, Carl. *One Move to Better Golf.* New York: Dell Publishing, 1990.

Mackenzie, Marlin M. *Golf: The Mind Game.* New York: Dell Publishing, 1990.

Mangrum, Lloyd. *Golf: A New Approach.* New York: McGraw-Hill, 1949.

Middlecoff, Cary. *The Golf Swing.* New York: Prentice-Hall, 1974.

Murphy, Michael. *Golf in the Kingdom.* New York: Dell Publishing, 1972.

Nelson, Byron. *Shape Your Swing the Modern Way.* New York: Golf Digest, 1976.

Nichols, Bobby. *Never Say Never.* New York: Fleet Publishing, 1965.

Nicklaus, Jack. *My 55 Ways to Lower Your Golf Score.* New York: Simon and Schuster, 1962.

———. *Play Better Golf—The Short Game and Scoring.* New York: Simon and Schuster, 1981.

———. *Play Better Golf—Short Cuts to Better Scores.* New York: Simon and Schuster, 1983.

Nideffer, Robert M. *Athletes Guide to Mental Training.* Champaign, Ill.: Human Kinetics Publishers, 1985.

Novak, Joe. *Par Golf in 8 Steps.* New York: Prentice-Hall, 1950.

———. *Golf Can Be an Easy Game.* New York: Prentice-Hall, 1962.

Palmer, Arnold. *My Game and Yours.* New York: Simon and Schuster, 1963.

Platte, Jules. *Better Golf Through Better Practice.* Englewood Cliffs, N.J.: Prentice-Hall, 1958.

Player, Gary. *Golf Begins at 50.* New York: Simon and Schuster, 1988.

Rees, Dai. *Dai Rees on Golf.* New York: A. S. Barnes, 1960.

———. *Putting Made Easy.* New York: A. S. Barnes, 1961.

Rosburg, Bob. *The Putter Book.* New York: Cornerstone Library, 1963.

Saunders, Vivien. *The Golfing Mind.* London, Eng.: Stanley Paul and Co., 1984.

Smith, Horton, and Taylor, Dawson. *The Secret of Perfect Putting.* New York: A. S. Barnes, 1961.

Snead, Sam. *How to Play Golf.* Garden City, N.Y.: Hall Publishing Company, 1946.

———. *Sam Snead on Golf.* New York: Prentice-Hall, 1961.

———. *The Driver Book.* New York: Cornerstone Library, 1963.

Sullivan, George. *The Champions' Guide to Golf.* New York: Fleet Publishing, 1966.

Toski, Bob. *The Touch System for Better Golf.* Norwalk, Conn.: Golf Digest, 1971.

———. *Golf for a Lifetime.* New York: Golf Digest, 1981.

Trevillion, Paul. *The Perfect Putting Method.* New York: Winchester Press, 1971.

Vaile, P. A. *Putting Made Easy.* New York: Reilly and Lee, 1935.

Wind, Herbert Warren. *The Complete Golfer.* New York: Simon and Schuster, 1954.

Wiren, Gary. *The New Golf Mind.* New York: Simon and Schuster, 1978.

Zaharias, Mildred Didrikson. *Championship Golf.* New York: A. S. Barnes, 1948.

Recommended Videos

The Biomechanics of Power Golf, Dr. Gideon Ariel.
60 Yards In, Raymond Floyd.
Neuromuscular Training/Sybervision, Al Geiberger.
The Bobby Jones Instructional Series/Sybervision, Bobby Jones.
Priceless Golf Tips, Volume One, Lee Trevino.
Priceless Golf Tips, Volume Two, Lee Trevino.
Priceless Golf Tips, Volume Three, Lee Trevino.

About the Authors

BOB FORD is the head professional at Oakmont Country Club. Recognition of his talent and overall golf knowledge includes:
- 1986 Tri-State PGA Horton Smith Award
- 1987 Tri-State PGA Teacher of the Year
- 1980, 1982, 1984, 1987, and 1990 Tri-State PGA Player of the Year
- 1985 National PGA Merchandiser of the Year
- 1987 National PGA Club Professional of the Year
- 1988 National PGA Club Professional Player of the Year
- 1988 National PGA Stroke Play Champion

Bob Ford has played in two U.S. Opens and four PGAs. He was a member of three PGA Cup teams and an instructor at PGA business schools and national golf education seminars.

DICK BEACH played the number one position on Yale University golf teams in the late 1940s. In the 1950s he had a handicap of two below scratch and held a number of course records with scores in the mid-sixties. Today, he plays at Pine Valley Golf Club, Oakmont Country Club, and Cypress Links Golf Club.